The War on Drugs: An Old Wives' Tale

Christine D. Shuck

Copyright ©2013 by Christine D. Shuck
Revised: November 2017

All rights reserved. Except as permitted under the U.S. Copyright Act of 1976, no part of this publication may be reproduced, distributed, or transmitted in any form or by any means, or stored in a database or retrieval system, without the prior written permission of the author.

Introduction

It was a sunny, beautiful day in late November. The sky was blue and there were just a few wispy promises of clouds high in the sky. I stood barefoot in the driveway, our two-year-old daughter in my arms. She cuddled against me, still drowsy from napping in the car.

It did not play out as you see on television. They did not come with their jackboots and battering rams. They did not break down our door or throw us to the floor, handcuff or arrest us. They did not draw their guns or shout at us, and the neighbors would only have known something was amiss if they were actively watching outside. The fact that they did not do any of those things did not make us any less terrified on that Monday in late November 2008, just a few days before Thanksgiving, when the Clandestine Lab

Task Force raided our basement marijuana-growing operation.

Welcome to the drug war.

By the end of our two-year-long experience, we had lost more than $30,000 in income and legal fees, struggled to keep our home and family intact, and were forced to declare bankruptcy. But our family is still together – and we still have our home. We continue to rebuild ourselves financially and emotionally – together – because of this I consider our family to be one of the lucky ones.

Each day, across this nation, hundreds of thousands of people are being arrested, threatened with imprisonment, losing their jobs, their homes, and personal belongings. They are being labeled criminals, their constitutional rights are being violated, and their families are ripped apart.

Between 2001 and 2010, there have been 8.2 million arrests for marijuana, 88% of those for *just* marijuana, no other drugs, weapons or violations.

Over 750,000 people in the United States are currently incarcerated for varying degrees of marijuana possession while murderers, rapists, and pedophiles often walk free due to 'overcrowding.' While Ponzi schemes earn house arrests and visits to country club prisons, untold thousands of children are suffering in one-parent households or find themselves at the mercy of an inadequate foster care system when their fathers and mothers are incarcerated. Drug task forces and police officers are allowed to confiscate possessions of our nation's citizens and call it justice-putting the onus of proof on the citizen if they ever hope to have the items or monies back.

Except for our names, Dave and Christine Shuck, I have changed all the names in this book. I did it to protect the innocent ... and the guilty ... I'll let you decide which is which.

This book is about our experiences in the two plus years that followed our bust as we progressed through the Cass County Adult Drug Court program. However, it is more than that-it is more than just an account of one family in a small Midwest town who decided to ignore the law. It is about one of the greatest ethical and legal battles plaguing this country in the last century.

In the two years that followed the bust-we would struggle to pay our bills. We would see first-hand the games and gross manipulations of our freedom done in the name of *justice* and *rehabilitation*.

In the last days of 2008, we found ourselves faced with a choice-we could go to prison or we could go through drug court. We entered drug court with great trepidation, with preconceived notions, and hard feelings, and found that life was not as simple as black and white, good or evil, or even courts and criminals. We walked away from the experience changed and with powerful lessons learned.

Welcome to the war on drugs.

A Beginning and an End

I met my husband Dave in 1984-in our sophomore year of high school. We both attended a small, private high school in San Francisco. The first year of school we spent together, we were lost in our own shy little worlds. He barely spoke to anyone-and chewed nervously on his jacket strings. I had been there a year, but I too was painfully shy. I would remain this way into my early 20s. When I dared to speak, it was to other outcasts like him-who were safe and friendly. By the end of that first year together, we had begun sitting at the same table and a quiet friendship had developed.

We were friends, just friends. However, as we headed into our junior year and we both began to grow out of our shells; I realized quite painfully that I was head over heels for this friendly, kind, and good-looking boy. I became one of a group of girls who spent an inordinate amount of time watching the boys play hacky sack in front of the large picture window during recess and lunch. Many of them were the 'popular' kids, and Dave stood on the outskirts of this group, still merging with my friends, but now spending his weekends with the other group at parties.

Much to my regret, our friendship during that time never progressed past the friend stage. After high school, I moved south to San Jose and got married, and soon after had a baby. A few years later that marriage ended disastrously. I connected with Dave once in 1995, invited him to dinner, but he was engaged to be married and made the appropriate excuses. Again, we lost touch. In 1997, I moved to Missouri, met and married another disaster and we divorced in early 2002. I was still licking my wounds from that experience when Dave discovered me on Classmates.com.

A few days before Christmas in 2002, he sent me an email wishing me a Merry Christmas and asking me how my life was. Sixteen years after high school and I felt like a teenager all over again, with butterflies in my stomach and love-struck eyes. My teenage daughter was very amused at my transformation.

After all, he was the one that got away. I had never had the guts in high school to say to his face, "I like you, a lot. Now would you please go out with me?" Over the years, whenever I would connect with old classmates I would always ask, "Have you heard from Dave Shuck? How is he?" Even then, I knew my voice gave me away. I was too interested, too desperate for news. The memory of him stayed with me, haunting me. He had been the first boy I had ever fallen for, hard, and I looked for him in other men's faces and in their smiles.

A thousand times I had regretted never telling him how I felt. It felt like an unfinished story. Yet here I was, 1,500 miles away, half a lifetime later, and it felt like high school all over again. We exchanged emails. We shared hours of long, soulful, amusing, reminiscent phone calls. He had been divorced for four years, no children, and I was rebounding from a traumatizing divorce and struggling to make ends meet as a single mom to my now-teenage daughter. Finally, after two weeks of nearly daily phone calls he admitted that he had been terribly disappointed to learn I was no longer in

California. "I was going to ask you out on a date," he said.

"What's 1,500 miles between friends?" I said, sounding far more confident than I felt. "I'd love to go to dinner with you. Come and see me, Dave." He laughed at first, but I repeated the offer, and then repeated it again. To my delight and terror, that is just what he did.

In late January 2003, he flew out for a week. It was unseasonably cold; the temperatures plunged to minus 10 degrees Fahrenheit, cold enough that my bathroom pipes froze and burst. I fell on the ice one morning and hurt my back. I spent the day on the couch in a haze of pain while he located the busted pipe in an unheated crawl space off of the main basement and helped the plumber repair it.

Before he left at the end of the week I said, "We're good people who have had plenty of awful things happen to us. We deserve some good. I'd like you to stay with me." Dropping him off at the airport and watching him fly away was one of the most difficult things I have ever done. I sobbed as I drove home. I knew I loved him still, that I had never really stopped loving him, not after all those years.

Some part of him must have felt the same way because two months later he packed up and drove to Missouri. He left behind all of his family and friends in San Francisco, the only place he had ever lived, to be with me. That was March of 2003.

It was tough finding a job at first. He did a couple of stints with bottom of the barrel call center positions before landing a job in the computer field as a repair technician working with industrial computers. Here he stayed while I quit my job, started my own business, and went back to school part-time. Six weeks into my first semester at UMKC, we learned I was pregnant. We married July 2, 2006 and our daughter P.E. was born October 4, 2006.

I could not have asked for a better father or husband. Dave was and still is committed, loving, and attentive. He has loved our little girl since the moment he saw her there on the ultrasound, snoozing inside me, and he was lost from the moment he first held her in his arms. I say this because I want it understood that, mistakes or not, or poor judgment on either of our parts, we are a family. We love each other deeply. When the proverbial crap hits the fan, we gather in, pull the edges away from the world, and center on what is important – our little family.

Computers had lost their allure long ago, but Dave stayed at his job. He stuck it out there for over four years before he found himself laid off at the end of May 2008. The fact that he had stayed in a job that he had come to despise, so that we would continue to have a dependable income and health insurance was a price he had been more than willing to pay. However, I had seen how it had pushed him into depression and constant anxiety as he fought to stay focused in a field he no longer loved, and in a job where he was degraded daily.

When the ax fell, I was actually relieved. "Take a month, even two or three," I told him. "You'll get unemployment and you need a break. Maybe now you can take some time for yourself and figure out what you want to do going forward." We tightened our belts, reduced our expenditures where we could, and turned our attention to family and home. I began working more hours with my cleaning business and at the professional organizing business I had started in 2007. I finished writing my first book on organizing and published it myself.

Two weeks after he lost his job Dave said, "I want to start a microbrewery and brew craft beer."

Brew beer? I don't even like the stuff. I can barely manage a sip or two out of politeness. But if that was what he wanted, then I would do what I could to make it happen. "Okay," I said. "Let's open a brewery."

Small problem ... money. Or, more specifically, a serious lack thereof.

It was my bright idea that helped build the walls which would later crash down on top of us. "Let's finish the basement out, create a secret room in it and grow marijuana," I suggested. "We can sell it and make enough money in a few years to come up with what we need to start the brewery."

In writing the paragraph above, I recall a television show, *Weeds*, which I watched obsessively for several seasons. The main character, Nancy Botwin, found herself a widow with no money and no real work skills, so she turned to selling dime bags of pot to make ends meet. One disaster after another, season after season, this woman's whole life was a hot mess. By the time Dave entered drug court, Nancy Botwin had set fire to her giant house in the suburbs, set metaphorical fires to most of her relationships, had a baby out of wedlock, and married her Mexican crime lord baby daddy. I just couldn't stop watching it – it was like a train wreck you can't tear your eyes away from.

We are not an episode of *Weeds*. I am not Nancy Botwin. Yet for a moment, looking at those words that I uttered, *"Let's finish the basement out, create a secret room in it and grow marijuana,"* it all seems so ridiculous, so completely asinine that now, I cannot believe I suggested we do it.

But I did suggest it, and Dave agreed to do it. We finished out the basement and created the secret room, dubbed Ground Zer' by the police. We bought the lights, rockwool, bags of Miracle Gro and all kinds of high-end fertilizers. Everything we needed to promote growth, encourage flowering, and eventually grow enormous buds of sticky, stinky, money-making, stupor-inducing splendor. We put in an air conditioner to reduce the high temperatures caused by the bright lights, a carbon filter and an ionizer to reduce smell. After a few months, we managed to reduce the smell to the immediate area, where no one but us would have reason to venture. We even entertained guests during this time-*non-smoking* guests, that is.

Nearly all of our family and friends are non-smokers. Dave, on the other hand, had been smoking since he was a teenager. He had only stopped once he moved to Missouri due to the lack of a good connection or high-quality product. My husband can be a bit of a snob at times. He enjoys micro-brewed beer and expensive, high-end weed. As for me, I am a writer, with a strong, type-A personality.

I run two businesses of my own, manage our finances and typically have a smorgasbord of household, craft, and writing projects underway simultaneously. Smoking weed interfered with all of my commitments. When high I cease to be able to operate simple machinery, such as a microwave, and my productivity comes to a screeching halt. My internal barriers, thin as they already are, come down and I say whatever is on my mind, inevitably embarrassing or harsh. I don't like how it makes me feel, so my sampling of the product was, and still is, a rare and unusual occurrence.

We made a very nice, high-end weed come out of our basement. Kush and White Widow; both strains were mild tasting yet strong. They easily sold at a price of $4,000 per pound, no haggling, and no problems.

Before I get too far, I also want to dispel the notion that we actually made *money* at this enterprise, because in the end, we lost thousands of dollars. When it all shook out, we probably made one dollar for every ten dollars we lost. Thousands of dollars in equipment were lost on the day of the raid, and we paid at least $30,000 more in raised utility bills, lawyer fees, and court costs before it all shook out.

This is also not some kind of a treatise on how the system 'done us wrong,' nor is it intended as a forum to brag about our law-breaking ways. It is an account of how we, Dave and I, became involved in the production of marijuana, how we were caught, and what happened afterwards. If it causes you to question the system or wag your finger at your kids as a warning of what happens to those kind of people, that is your decision. Think what you want, believe what you care to believe; learn what you will from our lessons ... if there even is one.

I also need to make clear how *long* growing marijuana takes when you are first starting out. Some of the seeds took forever to sprout, the germination rate was horrendous, and I began to wonder how old the seeds we used were. We were hit with a host of other problems ... heat issues, smell issues, male plants (very bad) and finally, these small flies that ate our delicate plants from the root up. Our harvests, when they occurred, were sad, pitiful affairs and the electric bill quickly doubled. By November 2008 we had managed one and a half good harvests, with maybe two to two and a half pounds of dried product. We had finally figured out a cycle of cloning, learned to control our pest problem, and were about to clone a new batch when disaster struck.

It was less than a week before Thanksgiving 2008 and we had just moved out our first real harvest of product to the buyer. We had paid some bills and had cash stashed away. Not a lot of cash, but enough to get by for a while. Dave had just returned with a brand-new set of lights that promised to conserve energy while making those money-making plants grow like mad. A friend was visiting; he was going to help us with painting in return for Dave's help re-wiring parts of his house the week before. We walked outside to unload the lights when three black SUVs screeched to a halt in front of our house. One pulled in behind our friend's truck, the other behind our van, and the third blocked the entire exit to the driveway.

A tall bald guy came striding up to my husband and said, "Dave Shuck? Still running a cleaning business out of your home?" He said it with a sneer, as if he was sure the answer was "no." We later learned that people use things like cleaning businesses as a front for laundering drug money. I actually did own and run a housecleaning business at that time. For that matter, I still do.

My husband must have nodded or said something in the affirmative in response to the officer's question, but mainly he was staring in horror at the badge the guy was flashing. "Well, I've got bad news for you, Dave. We've come for your plants."

Dave turned to me and said, "Honey, I'm going to prison." I love my husband, I really do, but I had forgotten how he was wired – tell the truth and obey police at all times. In this situation, it was suboptimal. His response was a dead giveaway that we were up to exactly what they were hoping we were.

The bald man stepped closer, as did the other men, ringing my husband and cutting me off from him. They focused on him as their main target, honing in on him as the weaker link in this situation. The head guy made a broad gesture, pointing toward the other middle-class houses and manicured lawns that surrounded us on all sides, "Let us in and your neighbors don't have to know that anything is wrong. We are not going to call DFS and we are not going to arrest you. We just want your plants." He smiled, "We'll be in and out of here in less than an hour."

I would like to think that I would have handled it differently. I know that the 'coulda woulda, shoulda' scenarios haunted me as they ran through my mind for weeks and months afterwards. I kept imagining how I would have stood my ground and acted confused. Maybe backed up fast, gone inside, and locked the door behind me. I could have asked for their warrant, or even told them to get off my property. Something, *anything* but say what Dave had said. I would have tried to buy us enough time to clear everything out. It would not have been that hard. If they had come by a few days earlier, they would have caught us with at least one pound of marijuana dried and ready for sale. If they had come by a few days later, they would have caught us with 48 new clones.

    That day in November was the start of a surreal world we would find ourselves in over the next two years. My husband, terrified beyond measure at the thought of losing our child to DFS, had signed a form allowing them to enter our house and showed them the grow room. He did this without reading what he was signing or asking if they had a warrant. By the time I thought to ask if they had a warrant, they had already been inside the house and seen the grow room. The man in charge, Jay Flight, said, "No, we don't. If we need to get that, we can. We will return with a DFS worker and I can't promise you won't be arrested."

I nodded, "I understand your threat; go ahead with what you are doing."

He smiled, "It's not a threat."

In my world, when you say that you will bring in the Department of Family Services and imply that there could be arrests, you are threatening me. However, the point was irrelevant; it was far too late for me to do anything but cooperate.

We learned quickly, albeit too late, that it had been a simple fishing expedition. What the police refer to as a "knock and talk." They had been staking out a hydroponics store in Kansas City for nearly a year. They followed Dave from the hydroponics store that day after they observed him purchasing the high-intensity grow lights. We were just another pair of fish hooked by the Clandestine Lab Task Force. After entering the drug court program, Dave would meet many more snared in the exact the same way.

They took pictures, video even, then photographed and fingerprinted both of us. They bagged up the plants to send to the lab. As we watched the process, the head guy, Jay Flight, smiled at us, "I know, I know, it's kind of like getting your kids taken away from you." We both just looked at him and shook our heads.

"No, it isn't. Our daughter is upstairs and she is our child. These plants mean nothing to us compared to her." I said, wondering for the first, but not the last, time just what kind of people he was used to dealing with. Dave made noises of agreement behind me.

They did not arrest us that day, a fact for which I am very grateful. I would learn later that cops can and will lie to you and say whatever it takes to get your cooperation. They can make grandiose promises, pledging to not call Child Protective Services, the media, or arrest you, and then later do exactly that. We were lucky; they kept their promises that day and left with only the plants and the thousands of dollars in equipment and lights. We sat there, contemplated running like hell for the border, hugged our daughter, and tried to figure out what to do next.

The task force had removed 13 plants, ten of which were scraggly and sad, on the point of death, and less than 1/8 of an ounce of weed. They missed our stash of cash, but then again, they had not looked too hard for that. Mainly they were interested in the high-end equipment, the lights still in their boxes, and anything they could confiscate and immediately sell.

Long before the results were back from the lab and the warrant issued for Dave's arrest, Flight's group had sold our confiscated property at a police auction. I learned later that every penny of that money went back to fund the task force and that, in the case of this particular task force, there is little oversight or restrictions on how they spent that money. This is probably why they all drive sleek black SUVs and look so well dressed. No matter how the charges had played out against us, they would never have to return or even pay for the property they had confiscated.

Yes, I will admit it. It galls me. Essentially, it is legal thievery hidden behind that nondescript legal term – "asset forfeiture." Even if they never charged us, even if the lab tests had come back negative, they would not have had to return the equipment or reimburse us in any way. If they had found cash on the premises, it would have been up to us to prove that the money was ours legitimately (i.e., *not* drug money). The potential for abuse through asset forfeiture is extraordinary and I will discuss this in more detail later.

It is an incontrovertible fact that the War on Drugs is wrapped tightly around the issue of money. This task force, and its brothers in law enforcement, uses Asset Forfeiture as an excuse to confiscate belongings and cash from hundreds of thousands of people each year. Many of these people have not broken the law, but they still lose. If I hadn't already been convinced of this fact, I certainly was months after the raid as we were cleaning up the house in anticipation of visits by trackers- a type of police officer whose job it is to search drug court participants' homes and cars for illicit substances. We rented a storage unit to house the banned items, such as Dave's beer brewing system, our beer glass collection, beer T-shirts, memorabilia, and books on beer making. If these items had remained in our immediate home, they would have been subject to confiscation and eventual sale.

As we cleared out the basement, I noticed that the task force had left behind part of the hydroponics system. I pointed it out to Dave, remarking that it was strange they had not taken it. "They said it wasn't worth any money, so they weren't going to bother taking it." My husband explained. I did not believe him and said so. "Seriously," he insisted, "*they said* they wouldn't be able to get anything for it when they sold it so they left it."

This is what I mean when I say that the War on Drugs is more about making money and less about protecting people from the dangers of drugs. If the issue is to discourage people from producing drugs by confiscating the production equipment used, then that crappy little piece of plastic that a row of plants sat in should have been confiscated along with the other items. The fact that it, along with other items that had no 'resale value,' were left behind speaks very loudly to drug task force priorities – get it, grab what you can make money off of, and move on. It is not about stopping crime; it is about *making money*.

    In the week following the bust, we had found a lawyer and set an appointment. Our defense attorney was an ex-prosecutor, and his partner was an ex-drug cop. During our meeting the ex-drug cop was playing with his new wireless camera. He would wink at me and tell me to "smile for the camera." It seems that old habits die hard with cops; I was far from amused.

    They advised us to have our cars detailed. When we looked confused, they explained, "Pot smokers smoke in their cars." We shook our heads and told them we never did. "Well, you might transport pot in your car then." Again, we shook our heads no, that we never had. The two of them looked at each other, eyebrows raised, and I could tell they were not sure whether to believe us or not. If I could have seen inside their heads then I am sure there would have been a vision of two stoned idiots driving down the road, smoking a joint with our young child looking on from the backseat. Nothing could have been further from the truth.

They told us it would be $7,500 to represent both of us. We scrounged up $3,000 and agreed to begin making regular payments of $100 per month. Then we went home and, after P.E. was asleep, smoked the pot missed by the task force. By that point, my stress levels were so high that I indulged as well.

One week later, we began taking regular urine tests. Our lawyer advised us to do this. He hoped to be able to prove that the marijuana was for personal use only and indicated that we were clean or getting that way. I had smoked recently, several times shortly after the raid, and Dave had been smoking heavily for months. All of this was outside or in the garage, away from our daughter and usually after she was in bed for the night. We kept it away from her always, and to this day she has no idea what marijuana is or what a marijuana pipe looks like, as she has never seen it in use.

I say this because I want you to have a clear picture of our life. Ours is a middle-class home in a middle-class neighborhood where the biggest excitement had been a recent rash of break-ins when people were away at work. We have extensive flower gardens and raise fresh herbs and okra, squash and asparagus each summer. We are the people next door who always have a spare cup of sugar or an extra egg. I am in the habit of bringing fresh-baked cookies to new neighbors, and we swap recipes and gardening advice. For us, the worst thing you will see is a few days of rather long grass (that would be our *lawn,* not *marijuana*) when we are caught up in other projects. In other words, we are normal people, with decent cars; a well-cared-for child, and great neighbors in a quiet suburb south of Kansas City.

The marijuana cleared out of my system quickly. In less than a month, I was as clean as a whistle. Dave took longer, nearly three months to be exact. This was exactly what the lawyer had hoped for. Although the number of plants was enough to put us in the production category instead of just personal consumption, the party line had to be that we were growing it for personal use. "Look, see here, big time pot smoker, used to smoking a lot. He's from California, for Christ sake!" Which is not to say that everyone in California is a pothead, but let's face it: things are a little different out there and it was a good defense.

The lawyer advised us to enroll in a drug-counseling program. We went to Pathways and enrolled. We each had different counselors. After the initial assessment, my counselor advised that my program would entail ten individual therapy sessions and ten group therapy sessions. This meant I had to drive down to Harrisonville each week to see her, but I could go to the closer town of Raymore to attend the group sessions.

My one-on-one counselor was serious and rather dour at first as I struggled with the propaganda she presented to me. In particular, I struggled with the idea that any repeated use over any length of time is addiction. I simply could not agree with this premise. At one point, early on in our meetings I stopped in the middle of the exercise and asked, "After this many weeks I hope you will believe me when I say that I smoke pot rarely, if ever. Now here I am in this position – waiting to hear when we will face charges and whether there will be the possibility of prison. Surely you have met someone in my position before this."

She shook her head, "Never. Not once. And I've been doing this for 30 years." It blew me away. It also did set a new, altered tone for our meetings. As my story remained the same, and did not crack or reveal inconsistencies, I think she came to realize that I was telling the truth. Most of our subsequent visits were less tense and at times, even friendly, as I shared with her my impressions of the group sessions and the other attendees. She laughed when I compared attending group counseling to an interesting social experiment. Months later, when Dave began the drug court program, he would relay that the individuals in the Pathways group sessions were college professors in comparison with the drug court participants.

One particular encounter with this counselor stayed with me, however. It was our third or fourth scheduled meeting and I had been participating in a class online and then had to race down to Harrisonville.

I was running late, just five minutes or so, but I called and let the secretary know I was on my way. When I arrived, my counselor met me at the door with a sour look and said in a very confrontational manner, "If you are ever late for one of our meetings again, I will discontinue your treatment. The state requires you to meet with me for the full 45 minutes and not a minute less. Do you understand?"

I was tempted to walk out right then, but I was quite aware that these meetings might eventually help our case, so I apologized and then waited for her to escort me to her office. No regular counselor would have ever spoken to me like that. She did it in as rude and confrontational manner as she possibly could. Combine that with the fact that she regularly started our sessions five minutes late and ended our sessions at precisely one-half hour (15 minutes short of the "mandated meeting length") at nearly *every visit*, I saw her behavior as hypocritical, petty, and controlling.

She was telling me quite clearly that she was in charge and I had better toe the line. This type of behavior is endemic in the law enforcement and drug treatment world. I made note of each departure time from there on out – we never once met for a full 45 minutes. The way I see it, when you won't follow your own rules, you forfeit all respect for your authority. Her behavior was nothing more than posturing and a play for power.

The waiting stretched out interminably. Our lawyer told us that the laboratory that had received our plants was very behind in processing. So much so that it was late May before the tests came back positive for marijuana and a warrant issued. On May 26, 2009, they issued a warrant for Dave's arrest. Until that point, we had assumed they would charge us both. Instead they pursued charges against only Dave.

Despite this, I would not breathe easy until a full year had elapsed. In our county, the authorities have 12 months to charge an individual after discovering that a crime has been committed. I would later learn that Dave had begged the task force not to pursue charges against me. He told them that, while I had known about it, I had not participated in any part of the marijuana growing operation. This was partially true. He was in charge of cultivation and harvests, but I had been in charge of the finances.

His assuming the blame would enable us to survive the two years that would follow. If we had both been in drug court, we would have lost all possible income, our house, and any chance of maintaining a stable home and family life for our daughter during that time.

Although the court issued the warrant on May 26th, our lawyer did not learn of it until June 12th. He called us that Friday afternoon and advised Dave to keep his head down for the weekend. He also arranged for Dave to turn himself in on the Monday after Father's Day, post bond, and be released pending trial that same day.

Father's Day weekend was a mess; we were both terrified. The hammer had come down. I talked Dave into going out to a Father's Day lunch at Flying Saucer, a beer bar in the newly revitalized Kansas City Power & Light district. Neither of us knew what might happen the next day and we were worried and scared. All we knew was that the charges were for a Class B felony, intent to manufacture and distribute a controlled substance. It carried with it a possible sentence of five to 15 years. As frightened as we both were, I knew that I needed to give him some semblance of normalcy. We went to lunch, enjoyed the day as best we could, and cuddled up close in bed that evening.

One note of interest to the reader: of the 13 plants that the team had seized, only ten of them were reported. Keep in mind, ten of these plants had already been harvested and were scraggly and dying. We had kept them on hand to see if we could manage to wring a few clones out of the worn-out leaves while other three plants (the ones *not* listed in the team's report) were the healthy ones all set to be cloned into new plants. What ever happened to the other three plants? You can bet that neither of us decided to mention that discrepancy. I will leave it to you, the reader, to make up your own mind on how or why that discrepancy might have occurred or where those three plants ended up.

Our lawyer was still talking about drug court being an option, but was careful not to make grandiose promises – there was still the very real possibility that Dave could go to prison. On Monday morning, I drove him down to the county seat, dropped him off, and went to pull money out of the bank to cover bail. The bail had been set at $7,500 and the lawyer was able to negotiate with the court to allow us to post 10% of it directly to the courts. Five hours and $750 later, Dave was free on bond. Our next court date was set for July 20, 2009.

His brief few hours in jail were stressful for him and frightening when he related them to me. It took nearly two hours to process him in, with one of the officers, Good Ole Boy, taunting, "Oh, I surrender! I surrender!" in a falsetto before putting him into a holding cell with three other men. "Now don't tell them about those cigarettes I let you keep!" He walked away laughing.

The men inside looked Dave up and down and one asked, "You holding?"

"Holding what?"

"Cigarettes, asshole. Are you holding?"

Dave gestured at his empty pockets, "I don't even smoke cigarettes."

"Yeah, but are you *holding*?" When Dave continued to look confused the man clarified, "Do you have them up your *ass*?" When Dave said no, the man winked at the others, "Maybe we should search you anyway."

Never having been in the system, we both realized later they may have just been giving Dave a hard time, razzing him a bit to keep themselves amused while they waited. However, some of the crimes these men had committed were rather terrifying. The one that stands out, even now, was the man who took a pickax to a man who had, as he told Dave, "disrespected my woman while I was in the joint." A *pickax*...good Lord, we had entered a world filled with madmen.

By the end of the waiting, he had been called a cream puff, and the others had grinned as they commented how much they hoped he could have a sleepover with them that night.

The guards were just as bad, barking orders, engaging in little power plays and intimidation tactics that would have shamed their mothers. I still ask myself, who were the worse animals, the ones with the keys or the ones behind bars? One side had no power, and they were being reminded of this fact, repeatedly. As a result, the moment they had a chance, they acted out. The other side had the power, and used it, and abused it, *because they could.*

More than ever I was determined to keep Dave out of jail. This was not the place for him. Running like hell for the border was even discussed. "Whatever it takes," I promised him, "we will keep you out of that place."

Three weeks of agonized waiting. Our lawyer had promised to contact us as soon as he had heard from the prosecutor, but he heard nothing. We went into court on July 20th completely blind. Would they tell us that drug court was out of the question? Would they reduce the charge down to a Class C felony (simple possession)? Would the drug task force object to drug court as our lawyer believed they would?

I told my mother we both had meetings to attend and arranged for her to keep P.E. for a long weekend. We dropped her off on Sunday afternoon and returned home, putting the house in order and distracting ourselves with mundane tasks such as laundry and mowing.

We waited anxiously for our lawyer outside of the courtroom, not realizing he was inside.

When he did come out, he had surprising news for us. "The task force has given the thumbs up for you to attend drug court," he said.

"What?" I said. "I thought you said that never happens."

Our lawyer, who had extensive experience with other marijuana-growing operations the task force had busted, shook his head and said, "In all of my experience, in all of my years as a prosecutor and now as a defense attorney, they have *never* agreed to a recommendation for drug court. You are the first I've ever heard of."

Having the drug task force disagree with a recommendation for drug court was the norm, which didn't carry a huge amount of weight, since plenty of others had been admitted despite the task force's objections, but it was unusual. It was one of the many indicators we would have that our case was unusual from others in many crucial ways. It also gave me hope, albeit foolish and quickly dashed hope, that Dave's experience in drug court would somehow be easier as a result. It was not, but we would remain the anomaly in many ways throughout our drug court experience.

Dave went before the judge and the charges were read. The judge's eyebrows shot up when the prosecutor stated that the drug task force had no objections to drug court. It wasn't just a surprise to our lawyer, but to the judge as well. The result of that day in court meant an *opportunity* to possibly participate in drug court. Dave was instructed to meet with Sherrie, the coordinator for the program, to discuss his possible participation, as soon as possible.

Our lawyer explained the process of qualifying for drug court and advised Dave, "When you meet with Sherrie, simply explain that although you have been drug-free since November, *remaining drug-free from your addiction*," he took care to put special emphasis on those words, "continues to be a struggle for you, something you have to work at one day at a time."

We went home and Dave made an appointment to meet Sherrie first thing in the morning. The next day he went to his meeting and I dashed off to two cleanings and back home to prepare to teach an organizing class that night. As I got ready, Dave deluged me with details about his meeting. There was a laundry list of prohibited items that would have to be removed from the house and put in storage.

Prohibited items included any brewing equipment, any beer glasses, T-shirts, or other beer paraphernalia. No Sudafed,

Nyquil, prescription pain medication or alcohol of any kind, including mouthwash, was allowed.

Phase One of the program would be the most difficult. Sherrie explained that he would be required to call in to a hotline each day to find out the color of the day. His color would be green. How appropriate! Anytime the color of the day was designated green, he would need to report to either the sheriff's department or to an officer of the drug court and submit to a drug test.

He would be required to attend the drug court diversion program every day of the week except Wednesday and Sunday and he would also be expected to attend Narcotics Anonymous meetings three times a week. On his free days it was entirely likely he would also be called to perform community service on an as-needed basis. Phase One would last a minimum of eight weeks and during that time the drug court did not want Dave to have any kind of employment at all.

Dave was instructed by Sherrie to clear everything out of our house that was drug or alcohol-related. When it was all out of the house, she would do a walk-through. We rented a storage facility and moved it all out. The year before when we were planning on starting a brewery, we bought a 20-gallon professional grade brew system for R&D purposes.

When we learned prior to starting the drug court program that prohibited equipment was subject to confiscation if not removed from the premises, we immediately moved it to the storage unit. Thirty dollars a month for storage was a small price to pay for almost $10,000 in equipment.

Dave called the phone number Sherrie had given him and let her know we were ready. She was a small, muscular woman with the sharp, no-nonsense attitude I've seen in policewomen. Beneath the muted makeup and conservative hairstyle lay the steely resolve that propels them through the police academy and into a profession dominated by men. Dave had mentioned that she had served as a patrolwoman before transferring into the probation department.

She gave a cursory onceover of the house, pointed to a bottle of wine from a local winery and Pabst Blue Ribbon metal collector's tray we had missed, and I took special pains to show her my flower, herb, and vegetable seed collection. I had updated my website where it would clearly show these items for sale. She thanked me for showing her the seeds and giving her some forewarning and said, "If the trackers had seen these, they would have been on the phone in an instant to me." I assured her that we wanted to cooperate, but that this was a way I was hoping to make a little money to help us get by while Dave was in Phase One. "They may want to take samples to take back to the lab," Sherrie warned us.

"That's fine," I replied, "I will give them whatever seeds they need to test." It would turn out that the seeds were an issue that required *another* meeting of all the drug court officials. For some, it still remained unresolved on August 3rd, the day Dave pled guilty to the charges in exchange for being allowed into the drug court program. As he stood before the judge, there was some confusion with some of the other drug court officials regarding my selling seeds.

The judge looked impatient, "We discussed this already."

"Yes, your honor, but we didn't actually *vote* on it," one of the drug court officials in attendance said.

The judge pursed her lips in frustration, "Does your wife put out a catalog, Mr. Shuck?"

Dave dodged the question slightly, "She sells the seeds on her website, your Honor, and the seeds are all listed there." He put his head back down and stared at his shoes.

"Fine, fine. She understands she must submit any seeds for testing upon request and we've discussed this enough and agreed. It's done." The judge then took Dave's guilty plea and directed him to report to the program on Friday, August 7th. It would later be delayed a week due to a scheduling conflict. Dave first official day of drug court was Friday, August 14th, 2009.

We had officially been accepted into one of the most difficult, intensive, and long-term drug diversion programs in the country. If Dave could complete it successfully, the charges against him would be dropped and his records sealed. In 16 months, possibly more, possibly less, Dave would walk away from this with a clean slate and no felony conviction.

Phase One

Day 1 – 8/14/2009
Color: Yellow

Drug court began on Friday, August 14th, 2009. The day began with an appearance in front of a different judge who made sure to emphasize to all of the newbies how lucky they were to be allowed to do this program and assured them that he (the judge) was not born yesterday and would be watching them carefully.

After court, Dave's intake began. This consisted of meeting with a series of counselors and officers involved with the program. A great deal of probing questions and paperwork were involved. Then, after a meager slice of cold pizza, there was a mandatory visit to the park to play softball. To say that our family is not sports-minded is an understatement. It didn't help matters that it was 90 degrees out and Dave was in a suit.

Ever since Dave had been officially accepted into drug court, two weeks prior, we had wondered when the tracker visits would start. They had told us then that the visits could start anytime and that they would be at night, late at night.

We are early to bed, early to rise kind of people. It is an odd evening when we are not both in bed by 10:30 p.m. And as things go, of course, Dave had gone to bed and I had just gotten ready when the doorbell rang.

"Well, that figures," I grabbed the clothes I had just dropped at my feet. "Don't you dare open that front door until I'm dressed." One dog was already outside and the other I held with one hand securely around her muzzle to stop her from barking. A police officer was standing in our front entry. He had to be over six feet, possibly six foot four to my husband's and my shared height of five foot six. I assured him that our smallest dog, Dixie, did not bite, and added I was putting her in the garage to calm down. I was not sure if the officer would need to go through the garage but, if so, Dixie would offer little threat.

The police officer introduced himself as Officer Wheatfield. He asked us to show him around and we did. He didn't open up cupboards or snoop in our spices, although he did ask to look in the refrigerator for any beer. Despite the legality of alcohol, if you are involved in the drug court program you cannot consume or be around alcohol at all. This means no restaurants with bars, no one in the home can consume or have alcohol in the house or the cars, and Dave's beloved home brewing equipment had to be removed and put into storage. Officer Wheatfield talked with us and shared his thoughts on the subject of marijuana before administering the Breathalyzer and urinalysis tests. "Personally, I don't like the stuff, but soon it will be legalized and you all won't have the problems you are having now."

Huh, do tell.

The Breathalyzer reading was zero, as Dave had not had a drop of alcohol in over three weeks, and the pee test was negative for any drugs. It had been more than nine months since he had smoked. Officer Wheatfield said his goodbyes and headed off to the next house on his list. It was 11:15 p.m.

Day 2 - 8/15/2009
Color: Blue and Level Four

The next day was Saturday and the second day of drug court. Dave returned frustrated and depressed. "Today it was all about me," he said, "and how I couldn't take responsibility for my addiction or recognize I was an addict."

This was one of my bigger fears.

My husband and I aren't very good liars. Long ago we realized that it was far easier to tell the truth than to try and keep track of the lies. Consequently, we have become almost incapable of lying, which was one of the reasons we were in this pickle. Both of us believe, quite sincerely, that marijuana is not physically addictive and very rarely is it psychologically addictive. Therefore, we don't believe that one can become addicted to marijuana any more than you can become addicted to flan or ice cream. You might like the taste, smell, or how it makes you feel, but if you were stranded on a desert island tomorrow with no flan, ice cream, or weed, you would not suffer any physical withdrawals or be in danger of dying for lack of the substance.

I had seen Dave stop smoking pot quite abruptly when money was tight. He went for a space of over two years not smoking, prior to us growing, because it was simply out of the question to pay good money for it when we had a child. Yes, he'd get grumpy for the first couple of days. Pot gives most smokers a nice little mellow. Take that mellow away and all the emotions are right there at the surface needing to be dealt with. After a week, he would adjust and be back to normal.

In either state, smoking or not, Dave has done amazing tasks around the house – built a privacy fence, assembled raised planters, laid tile floors, and finished out the basement. His productivity, unlike the anti-pot commercials, was not affected by smoking. In fact, it often helped him stay in that productive groove that yielded so many wonderful results around the house.

I say all of this because, although I don't personally like the effects of smoking pot, I recognize that in many cases marijuana has helped center my husband and focus him more often than it has distracted him. Does that make me a co-dependent? Perhaps, although I honestly don't think it does.

Here he was on only Day 2 of drug court and the others were laying into him pretty severely. They called him an alcoholic, a junkie, and insisted that he was in denial. "Ah the arrogance of newbies," one of them said.

Here lies the rub. To get through the program and graduate successfully, (i.e., not go to prison) you have to go through a series of phases, participate in Narcotics Anonymous, and successfully complete their Twelve Step program. So, the question was struck, hard and cold, on the first day of NA. I asked my husband, "At what point will you just tell them what they want to hear? And how long can you stand to lie?"

Dave just nodded grimly. "Exactly."

We had both realized, on this second day of drug court, that it was not a matter of simply enduring the invasion of privacy or giving up our constitutional rights. It was a matter of learning to lie about our basic beliefs. And worse than that, he would have to lie *convincingly*.

In essence, we were taking our first steps into becoming what we considered to be immoral.

Day 3 – 8/16/2009
Color: Yellow

Dave's day off from drug court. A storm had rolled in, and it rained hard for hours from the wee hours of the morning until nearly noon. The chicken coop that Dave was planning on building would have to wait, and all of the holes he had already dug out were filled with muddy water. I transplanted 40 more strawberry plants and canned green beans.

We talked about drug court and addiction when he said thoughtfully, "I do think I will get some benefit out of this program. I'm examining my habits and I realize that I probably *do* abuse pot. When it isn't around, I don't particularly miss it. But when I have it I tend to smoke more and more of it as time goes by. On the first day I'll smoke a bowl. On the second day, I'll smoke two bowls. And it just keeps increasing from there."

The day passed without incident until Dave, on the phone with his brother-in-law, suddenly ended the call in a panic. He had forgotten to call in and check on his color. Every day, without fail, for the entire length of the program, you must call in and check the 'color of the day.' If your color is picked on a Sunday or holiday then you must go down to the county jail and drop a UA there.

The call-in time is from 7 a.m. to 5 p.m., and you must provide the UA between the hours of 9 a.m. and 5 p.m. So, in reality, you need to call in by 4-4:30 p.m. at the very latest. Unfortunately, Dave remembered at 5:35 p.m. It did not matter that the color was yellow and he would not have needed to drop; he had missed calling in. Just three days into the program and it was an automatic 24-hour stay in jail, executed immediately. His parole officer returned his panicked phone call and told him to report to jail right away.

Day 4 – 8/17/2009

Color: Unknown

This was Dave's first and hopefully last day in jail. He was in my thoughts when I closed my eyes that night and again the moment my eyes opened in the morning. I looked at the clock – 7 a.m.- he only had 12 more hours to go. Today was my first day at a new job and my mother would be arriving in a little over an hour to watch P.E. I got up, woke the kiddo, made breakfast, and then began the cleaning I had been too depressed to do the evening before.

All day I wondered when Dave would return. I knew it would be 24 hours from the time he was admitted into jail. But did that mean the minute he had walked in and surrendered, or 24 hours from when they had completed their intake and paperwork? Dave had left the house at approximately 6:10 p.m. on Sunday and he returned at 7:38 p.m. Monday evening to shrieks of welcome from P.E. and a long hug from me.

His time in jail had been uneventful. The officer who had done his intake had been concerned about Dave and kept asking him if he was okay. When the officer learned that Dave hadn't been in jail before he took some time and found a cell that contained non-violent offenders. It was a small kindness which meant a lot. Dave spent most of the day reading a Stephen King novel. A few minutes before 7 p.m. he called for a guard and reminded them he was only supposed to be in for 24 hours. They processed him through quickly and he drove straight home.

Day 7 - 8/20/2009
Color: Blue and Green

Dave woke in the middle of the night. "I dreamt that your mother became a tracker," he said. "We were living on a reservation and they were taking all of the children and pulling out their teeth to stop them from making little grass baskets. Your mom threw down the bag and we could hear the clicks of the little teeth and watched them spill onto the ground."

Dave is historically aware of his Cherokee roots and explained that, during the mid-to-late 1800s when the government tried to eradicate the otherness of the American Indian, they would often take the children away from their parents. They discovered that Cherokee mothers taught their children about their tribal heritage through songs and crafts. They would show their children how to weave grass baskets with their teeth and fingers while singing songs. Government officials sometimes had the children's front baby teeth pulled to keep them from weaving.

Later that day in group he talked about some of the nightmares he had been having. "Dude, ya gotta relax. Get some sleep; stop worrying so much," another drug court participant advised. Dave had been dreaming nightly of trackers and talking about them in group each morning.

Dave's color had come up, so he had to drop a UA that day.

Dropping a UA at the sheriff's office for the court meant (for men at least) that Dave had to raise his shirt high up on his chest, drop his pants and turn in a slow circle while the deputy watches. The last step is to grab his penis and pull it up, exposing his scrotum in order to show there is no pouch of clean urine hid anywhere on his body. Only then does the deputy hand him the urine cup and the deputy is required to watch as he urinates into it.

Drug court members had been caught trying to sneak in clean pee through a number of ways: the Urinator, douche bottles, even a vanilla bottle full of urine. Thus, the process for collecting a sample was rather intrusive.

Dave's days were filled with meetings with drug counselors, group sessions, general education, and other miscellaneous activities. I looked forward to evenings at home with him, but those hopes were quickly dashed when he informed me that frequent Narcotics Anonymous meeting attendance was also expected. We managed to find a good balance early on. He would return from Harrisonville's day program and pick up P.E. from daycare and fix dinner. We would eat at the table as a family and share any news of the day. He would drive to an NA meeting at about 7:40 and return by 9:15, just in time for bedtime rituals.

That night he returned from the NA meeting and said, "Well, today I said I was an addict."

"How did that feel?" I asked.

He shot me a look, "How do you think it felt? Try it out and see how it feels."

"Hi, I'm Christine and I'm an addict. I'm addicted to ice cream and chocolate." I said playfully. Dave just stared at me, not amused. "Okay, so how did *they* react to you saying it?"

"Oh, they loved it." He had been getting a full ration of crap at each meeting because he had refused to say he was an addict. This act of capitulation made his life easier in the meetings and seemed completely reasonable. Other NA members had explained that, even if he didn't agree with it, saying the words aloud was sort of a "fake it until you make it" mentality. Eventually, the hope is that the person will actually believe they are an addict. Until that point, some level of conformity is expected.

This also reminds me of a little factoid that Dave regularly mentions, "The id has no sense of humor, no sense of sarcasm. So if you say out loud, I am a loser then that is what the id hears and the unconscious comes to believe."

This is why positive affirmations can be so helpful. By saying positive thoughts out loud, you access that part of your brain that processes things so literally, turning those unconscious negative thoughts into positive ones.

So, while I rolled my eyes at the time at this act of conformity, I understood it. Dave had to take this step and show a level of accommodation in order to proceed forward personally and show conformity with the program.

Day 8 – 8/21/2009

Color: Blue and Green

Every Friday was court day for Phase One members. Each member would meet with the judge and she would speak with them personally. Dave had been advised by his counselors not to say, when she asked, that he was doing well. "The judge doesn't want to hear that things are going fine," they warned, "she wants to hear that you are struggling, but that you are making progress."

    He dressed, as he always did for court, in a dress shirt, pants, and shoes. He had a change of clothes in the car this time, in case there was mandatory softball that afternoon. He approached the bench and the judge eyed him, "Mr. Shuck," she said smiling slightly, "I have a philosophical question for you." Dave groaned slightly and looked properly miserable. "Do you believe that there are any *medical* benefits to smoking cannabis?"

    "For some people, yes ma'am, I do. However, I am not one of them. I tend to abuse it when I have it." His reply was straightforward and honest. The judge seemed surprised by his honesty and possibly taken aback as well.

    "I look forward to speaking to you again, Mr. Shuck." The next day he would hear that the judge had been very surprised to hear his honest response. It was a bit of a shock to her, and she commented to one of the other drug court officers that he was one of the first people in the program to actually answer honestly and not just tell her what she wanted to hear.

Our lawyer had relayed to us that many of the members of the drug court panel were intrigued with us. We were an oddity, they said, and they were all very curious to see how Dave progressed through the program. It seemed that, after only one week, we were still quite an odd and unique difference to the norm.

A couple of days before, we had gotten news that Pit Bull, one of the more vocal anti-drug participants in the program, had been pulled over in Kansas on an old warrant. One of the rules of drug court is that if a cop pulls you over, anywhere, you must immediately inform him that you are a participant in the Cass County drug court. She did, and was apparently asked to drop a UA. It came back dirty for prescription drugs. This apparently happened three weeks prior, but she said nothing to the other drug court participants, even led a meeting at NA and received her one-year drug-free pin. She claimed her husband gave her some medicine for a migraine and she took it without looking at it closely. The test results showed that she had taken three Tramadol.

Dave looked rather sad about this, despite the fact that the woman had given him such a hard time the first two days he was in the program. As she furiously chain-smoked on one cigarette after another she proclaimed him an alcoholic and a junkie who was in denial. When he pointed to her smoking she responded, "I *know* I'm a junkie and I *admit* I'm a hopeless addict."

Later that evening he would comment on how disappointed he was in her. "There are going to be a lot of failures, all around you, in this program." I pointed out. "Try not to let this get you down. You are going to be a success story to share with others!"

Day 9 – 8/22/2009
Color: Yellow and Blue

Dave had asked me a day or so before to please ask him each morning, right at 7 a.m., what the color of the day was. "If I'm not awake, wake me up so I can call in." I had promised him I would. At 7:08 a.m. I opened the door to our bedroom, and he was standing there by the bed, having just gotten up.

I smiled at him, "What's the color of the day?"

He smiled back, "I don't know, I'm going to go check right now." He returned a moment later and said, "Yellow and blue." He paused for a moment and joked, "Yellow and blue make green." I just rolled my eyes.

Dave was in a good mood that morning. He would be teaching Chi Gung at 12:30 p.m. to his fellow participants. When the counselors had learned about his martial arts skills during the intake, they had suggested that he might want to teach some classes to the others. He had agreed to this readily.

Not only would it give him some good points with the drug court officials, but Chi Gung is relaxing and would help him and the others regain a sense of calm and goodwill, despite the invasive practices of the drug court program. He was also tentatively approved to leave the county beginning in September to teach a class in Overland Park on Wednesday mornings at 6:30 a.m. for pay. It would mean approximately $40 a week, not much, but some amount of income was better than none. If the class was successful it would lead to more and he could possibly start a business teaching Chi Gung ... a far better option than going back into computers when his schedule at drug court allowed for more work hours.

Dave returned at almost five o'clock, looking exhausted and said, "We had to go on a Bataan Death March today. Three and a half hours through the wilds of Harrisonville."

Between eating healthy, home-cooked meals, no beer, no pot-smoking (and therefore no attacks of the munchies), and all of the exercise, my husband was already losing weight. I was slightly envious of this fact since I would have been quite excited to lose weight right alongside him.

Saturdays in drug court were basically "got to fill the hours somehow" days. At this point, only four people were Level One and required to attend on Saturdays. Their walk included wandering through a graveyard and taking rubbings of some of the headstones and trekking through fields of weeds and rundown farmland. I had been researching wild edible plants for my first fiction book *War's End,* and he remembered quite a few of the 'weeds' along the roadside and pointed them out to the others.

Day 13 – 8/26/2009
Color: Yellow and Green

Wednesday was Dave's day off from drug court. But it looked as if he would have to interrupt his plans for building the chicken coop long enough to drive down and submit a UA.

Drug court consists of four Phases and treatment at Cass County Psychological consists of three Levels. Dave would progress through these phases and levels in a typically concurrent pattern. He would begin in Level One and Phase One-and once he had reached Phase Four in drug court-he would be in the final stretch. During Level One of treatment, participants are required to be in Harrisonville at the diversion program every Monday, Tuesday, Thursday, Friday and Saturday from 9 a.m. to 4 p.m. No exceptions. Each Friday they must go before the judge, list the length of time they have been drug-and alcohol-free and report on their progress.

After a period of eight weeks the participant is allowed to phase up and more importantly, level up, giving them more free days in which to pursue employment or an education. The process of phasing up or 'leveling up' were dependent on not having any violations and appearing to be doing well in the program. 'Up-levels' were only allowed on the 1st Friday of the month. Since Dave had entered the program on the 2nd Friday of the month, it meant that if he stayed violation-free, he would qualify for Phase Two and Level Two on October 2nd. However, he had received a violation on Day 3 (forgetting to call in for the color of the day) and so that had pushed his 8th week to the 9th of October.

Would he have to wait until November 6th to phase up to Phase Two? Our concerns were mainly financial. My income through cleanings and my part-time job were not enough to cover our expenses, we were falling short by over $1,200 each month and that was on top of no longer being able to pay our credit card bills (an additional $1,500). Our home phone rang constantly from 8 a.m. to 8:30 p.m. every day of the week, despite our explanations to the credit card companies of our lack of funds.

To say that we needed Dave to "phase up" to Phase Two so that he could get at least a part-time job was an understatement. And the sooner that happened, the better. He expressed his concerns to a counselor and was told that, barring any further problems or violations, it was entirely possible that he could "phase up" in his seventh week, on October 2nd. What a relief! He could begin earning an income in October! We were, if possible, even *more* determined to remain sanction-free so that could happen.

Day 14 – 8/27/2009
Color: Orange and Blue

Dave returned from his day in Harrisonville a tad disgruntled. "They keep telling us they want the truth from us, right?" he began, quite out of sorts, "But they asked us today, 'How many of you look forward to coming here every day?' I was the only one who told the truth and said 'No' and they jumped my ass about it. I know for a fact that several others loathe having to be here, but *they* just nodded and towed the party line." He adopted a mock falsetto, "Oh thank you for saving me from myself, I just love coming here!" He shook his head. "It was disgusting. And all day they rode my ass about it; not just the counselors, but *everybody*."

The role of the observer is difficult. I could see with clarity his point but also the larger machinations at work here. The program was designed to, among other things, break each individual down. To *show* them how their lives are out of their control and *bend* them into conforming to the will of the court and the will of law. And whose will are we talking about? We are talking about the will of those in power, those in control.

In reality, honesty is neither expected nor accepted in this paradigm. Conformity is.

I don't say this out of resentment or frustration. The situation was what it was and I recognized it. I could see the trap coming because, while I am a *part* of this, I am not in the *middle* of it. It gave me perspective and it also was a warning. Over and over for me the same question presented itself – how could I best support Dave through this process? How could I be the person he could come home to and share his frustrations and news with? How could I also be a support system, perhaps even a guide through the more difficult days?

Our goal was to survive drug court with our family, our sanity, and our finances as intact as we could make them. We looked at the program as a far more attractive alternative to incarceration or becoming fugitives.

The perspectives we have when we are smack dab in the middle, rather than viewing from the sidelines, are very different. I imagine that's why they have umpires at games. They are removed from the action and can see more than any individual player in the game. They can call foul where others are unaware of the bigger picture or when something not quite in the player's line of sight occurs. I realized how different my perspective was. For me, the admonition that the drug court officials 'wanted the truth' was a huge warning sign. But for Dave, sitting there with meth addicts and ex-crack dealers – the view was a little more muddled. Pair with that the startling fact that some of the counselors were ex-addicts themselves with little formal training other than their dark experiences with addiction and you had a cocktail for disaster.

Telling the truth was the last thing Dave needed to do. But I couldn't say that to him. Instead I would have to discuss human nature-the tendency toward pack behavior in situations such as this-and gently touch on the anachronistic behaviors of humans. We say one thing and mean something completely different. But I saved the discussion for another day and focused on dinner and family. We all needed that familiar routine to keep us distracted from these greater frustrations.

After dinner he left to attend an NA meeting and I waited for his return. The minutes ticked by and I began to worry. His curfew was at 10 p.m. and it was 9:40 p.m. when he finally walked through the door. He explained that a new guy had showed up at the meeting. He was addicted to Hydrocodone and had yet to become clean. Dave received his 30-day key ring that night and the guy asked to talk to him after the meeting.

"How did you make it 30 days?" he wanted to know.

Dave hadn't had the difficulty leaving alcohol or weed behind, but he answered the best way he knew how. "I didn't make it 30 days. I made it one day at a time. And if that's too much for you right now, hey, that's okay. Make it one hour, then make it two, and go from there." He gave the guy his phone number and told him it was okay to call him if he needed someone to talk to.

I was happy for Dave, because I knew it made him feel good to help someone else. We watched our show and went to bed. Just as we were falling asleep, the doorbell rang, sending our dog Dixie into a loud barking fit. We pulled on our clothes and went to the door. I recognized the guy; it was same one who had yelled at everyone to be quiet when there was even an inkling of a murmur in the courtroom. He was also the one who had set Dave up in the holding cell by suggesting that Dave had cigarettes.

He was a small man, wiry and shorter than us. This is saying a lot, because Dave and I are both 5'6", so we're on the smallish side (height-wise at least) ourselves. We let him in and he looked at the living room, remarking in surprise, "Well, you have a really lovely home here." He looked over at me after a moment and asked, "So, are you Dave's mother?"

I was so shocked I didn't know what to say at first. I looked at Dave for a moment and turned back to Deputy Good Ole Boy and said, "I'm Dave's *wife* and I'm a year younger than he is."

Deputy Good Ole Boy had the common sense to apologize and give a flimsy excuse, "Oh, I'm sorry, I'm not wearing my glasses."

The words spilled out before I could stop them, "Well, I guess you'll need them in this house." Even now, as I write this, I am still so unbelievably irked. I said a few choice words after he left. None of them were polite and certainly none of them repeatable.

Deputy Good Ole Boy asked Dave how long he had been in drug court and wanted to know how he was doing in the program. "I'm doing okay," Dave said, "I'm very motivated to get through the program as soon as possible to everyone's satisfaction."

"Well, don't forget this program is for you," replied Deputy Good Ole Boy. "It's designed to improve your life and choices." I could see that Dave was biting his tongue at that, so I tried to add my assistance.

"When Dave says 'to everyone's satisfaction' that includes our own. We are both committed to learning from this experience." I cut in before Dave could say anything more.

Deputy Good Ole Boy looked over at me and nodded approvingly, "You have a strong, supportive woman here, Mr. Shuck."

Dave put his arm around me and smiled. I plastered a polite smile on my face, even as I wondered how this guy could be so dumb and still hold down a job. Due to his distinctive Southern accent I named him Deputy Good Ole Boy, but my first name for him (all during the drug court program) was Deputy Dumbass. I guess I'm not a particularly forgiving soul.

Deputy Good Ole Boy did a quick look-through of our house, and as he viewed the former grow room in the basement (now used for storage), turned and asked me if I had known about the marijuana-growing operation. I simply smiled and asked, "Can I take the fifth on that?"

As I had done earlier for him, Dave jumped in and rescued me. "She knew, but it was all me doing the growing; she never even came down here." Deputy Good Ole Boy went on to ask how Dave had been caught. "They followed me from the hydroponics store where I had been buying more energy-efficient lights."

When Deputy Good Ole Boy asked how they had gotten in, Dave answered, "They told me if I let them in, they would take the plants and equipment. If I made them get a warrant, they would take my child away from me." He shrugged and continued, "My child is far more important to me, so I let them in."

As we walked back up to the main level the deputy made an attempt at sounding sympathetic. I shrugged and said, "It is what it is. We don't waste our time blaming others. We did what we did and now we are paying the price. It's as simple as that." Dave heartily concurred.

And that is the way we see it. This isn't a pity party or a harangue on the system. We broke the law with a full understanding of the implications. Wrong or right, we did what we did and we accept the consequences of our actions. That's what mature adults do. If we don't like the law, then we need to work to change it. If we cannot change it, we need to move to a place where such a thing is acceptable or cease doing the activity. There are many laws on the books I do not agree with. There is an alarming trend toward the 'nanny state' we see in countries like Britain that I do not agree with. That said, the situation we found ourselves in – it was what it was and we understood and accepted it. We had screwed up, and now we were paying the price.

Deputy Good Ole Boy administered the Breathalyzer test a second time (having already forgotten that he had done it when he first walked in the door), looked over the flower and vegetable seeds I had lying out ready for sale, petted our dogs, and left. It would be past midnight before I fell back asleep.

Day 15 – 8/28/2009
Color: Green

Friday was court day. Dave was the last of the Phase 1 participants to be seen by the judge and as he approached the bench, she unleashed her fury on him. "I read in this report," she said, waving the paper in the air, "that you are not taking this program seriously. I read that you are refusing to admit your addiction and seem to think far too much of yourself. Give me one good reason why I shouldn't send you to prison right now for the full 15 years."

Dave gaped at her, completely blown away by the assault. "But I *have* admitted that I'm an addict, in group and at NA. I'm doing everything I can to cooperate, to participate."

She raged on, ignoring his response and furiously questioned his assertions that the cultivation of pot was permissible by law in some municipalities, namely Oakland and Santa Cruz, California. The idea of it being allowed at all, anywhere, seemed to rankle her no end. At two different points in the conversation, completely infuriated with him, she told Dave that he was "no different than a child rapist."

He was shaking with fury when he related the experience to me that evening. By the time he finished *I* was shaking with fury as well. I sat down and wrote the following letter:

Dear Ms. Baker-

I am more than aware of the proper title to address you with, but I see no reason to further the lie that I either respect you or find you honorable.

You will not receive this letter until my husband, Dave Shuck, has successfully completed your program and his record has been sealed. I have no interest in jeopardizing that certain future by saying to you what I think of you until then.

Today (August 28th, 2009) you swore at my husband, sneered at him and degraded him because you apparently did not bother to fully read the report given to you by Dave's counselor. If you had bothered to progress beyond sentence #2 you would have seen the glowing recommendation, she had written about him. Two full paragraphs, in fact, of how much he has grown and learned and committed to change in barely two weeks of Phase One.

But you didn't bother to read it, and instead unleashed such idiotic and undeserved fury on him that he was still shaking with emotion that evening telling me about it.

In particular, you said something that I find heinous and completely unacceptable. You said that his crimes were as bad as raping a child. You said it twice. To say how unforgivable that was to me I must give some kind of explanation first.

Dave and I met in high school and I fell in love with him when I was fifteen years old. He was kind to me; he was my friend when I was a social outcast, and a person so shy that to this day I barely remember my classmates' faces (I was too busy staring at the carpet). We lost touch after graduation. I married young and had a daughter. Eventually I divorced my husband and moved to Missouri with my young daughter. Six years after that Dave located me through Classmates.com while I was reeling from a disastrous second marriage and divorce. You see, my second husband had been a pedophile and he had molested my daughter for nearly four years before she told me what was happening. We called the police the very night I learned the truth and my husband was arrested the next day. The day after that he was released on bond and he walked free for a full year while awaiting judgment. During that year he found another victim, a little six-year-old girl to groom. No one bothered to protect her.

That monster was finally, finally sent to prison, despite the failings of the system (your system). Without my tenacity he would have walked free within months. No prosecutor or judge gave a damn about justice then. Everyone wanted to make a deal and drop or consolidate charges. In the end there was just me and my friend driving hundreds of miles and showing up at parole hearings in Farmington, Missouri. We were unbelievably lucky that the bastard had the good grace to drop dead in prison 10 months before your system would have released him and given him carte blanche to continue his recidivist ways. It was clear to anyone paying even the slightest amount of attention at the parole hearings that he would most assuredly offend again.

Dave is not the same as that. Not even close. The thought of his being labeled a child rapist wounds (and angers) me in ways I cannot describe, not in words, not on paper. When he found me, visited, and then moved across the country to be here with me, he revived my belief in in men and in life in general. He healed my heart and showed me that there are still those who can be trusted. He helped teach my eldest Algebra on a white board in the basement, listened to her, and was a patient, loving father figure to her. My husband, my partner, and my love, is NOT the equivalent of a child rapist. He never could be. Instead he is an adoring father, loving partner, and an invested, active member of the community. You are so blind, so jaded by idiots and monsters and meth heads that you cannot even conceptualize what a good and kind person looks like any longer.

 Shame on you. You have so much power over us. You have such power over him. And you misuse it. You wield your power with ignorance instead of knowledge, with pre-conceived conclusions instead of real, honest inspection. Shame on you. All you have done today is remind us that you have the power and that we must do whatever we have to do – lie, capitulate, and even deny our own beliefs, so that you have the final word. In exchange we hope to survive this process with at least some of our freedoms intact. That's the lesson we learned today. It's probably the same lesson we will get to learn again and again and again for the next 466 days.

And that's fine. We understand we screwed up. The law of the land, this land here in this state, was broken and we will take our licks. We will dance to your tune and smile and thank you like dogs licking an abusive master's hand. And here in this state especially, Dave is committed to never breaking those laws again. So, you can consider your program a success. Despite the gross idiocy of those involved, I am thankful for a program that keeps my husband where he belongs … with his wife and his child, as a productive member of society.

But think twice before you label someone a child rapist. Because until you've lived through learning you were married to one, you'll never know how wrong a label like that is to someone who is so undeserving of it.

One final comment that I hope you will consider as you continue sitting in that illustrious seat and wearing those robes. I think that if you aren't going to fully read the reports in front of you, then you might consider apologizing for not bothering to do your homework and then jumping to the wrong conclusions. Or are judges so high and mighty that they no longer make mistakes like the rest of us ignorant, law-breaking civilians?

It made me feel better to write the letter. I never did send it and she will probably never read it ... unless she happens to be holding this book. And if she is reading this? Fuck you, Judge Baker, because you are the real problem here, not my husband.

Day 16 - 8/29/2009
Color: Green

"They were planning on doing collage again today," Dave mentioned before he left. "I asked them if there was anything else, *anything* else that we could do instead. When Sonia asked why, I told her, 'We aren't in kindergarten, you won't trust us with scissors and the glue sticks are all numbered to make sure we give them back.'"

I, in turn was dreading a party that I had agreed to attend. It was a princess party for a four-year-old playmate of P.E.'s. The child had certain mannerisms that seemed contagious – lovely things like hitting, kicking, and making these awful animal grunting noises. Her mother and I hadn't been on a play date in well over a month, due in part to her learning of our "legal troubles" and suggesting that she "wasn't comfortable" having play dates at each other's houses. A handful of awkward meetings in local parks and we both just stopped calling each other.

And after watching my child grunt like an animal when she didn't get her way, or hit at me or her dad, I figured it was all for the best. I really didn't like her picking up on the other child's mannerisms.

To be completely honest, I agreed to go to the party because I was afraid P.E.'s party, which was coming up in just five weeks, would be rather lean on children if I didn't invite the little beast. I figured if I went to her party, her mother would feel guilted into coming to P.E.'s party. A sad excuse, but that was the reason I gave myself as I clicked the "Accept Evite" button.

The truth is that I woke up mad that morning. Mad at our circumstances, mad at the judge, mad at my fair-weather sort of friend for being a coward, mad at that damned stupid deputy for making me wonder just how old I looked to people ... and mad that I actually cared what they thought!

It was hard to go to that party. Harder still to smile and laugh and act as if I didn't have a care in the world. I was worried about Dave, who had a headache for the fourth day in a row. I was worried about money, and P.E., and my own self-worth, and the credit card companies who called incessantly.

If you had met me that day you wouldn't have guessed it. I made conversation, talked about gardens and dogs, and took pictures of the kids and promised to send copies to my friend. I was the perfect mother, a pleasant person to talk to, and I looked relaxed and at ease. By the end of the day I felt as schizophrenic as the court system. How could I be two extremes and not be a complete wreck?

Every day since Dave's participation in drug court began, I told myself that I needed to be strong. I needed to be supportive and steady and not lose it emotionally. I needed to be the person my husband so desperately needed me to be – his rock, his support system, his haven from the lunacy he had to deal with at least five days a week. But part of me wondered how in hell I was going to manage to keep this up for 16 more months.

Day 17 - 8/30/2009
Color: Orange and Blue

Now that Pit Bull was out, the focus would hopefully shift away from Dave for a while. The color of the day seemed to indicate a lessening in their scrutiny of us as other people drew their attention more and more.

The headache that Dave had suffered from for the past four days had transferred over to me and I was struggling with it. I wanted to write, clean my desk, even work in the yard – but my head was pounding in protest.

Dave was feeling good. Not having to drive to Harrisonville to pee in a cup probably helped his mindset. He baked biscuits and mowed the lawn. Later friends came over, desperate for help in replacing a hard drive. We whiled away the afternoon while Dave installed updates and an operating system. While the men chatted, my friend and I ran to a crafts store to get supplies so that I could finish Danielle's birthday quilt.

As usual, she wanted an update on "the situation" and I filled her in on the many details since we had last chatted. Some of the attitudes that she and her husband had were rather at odds with ours. But they seemed like good people who made entertaining conversation, and our children played well together, so I usually ignored the infrequent gaps in methodology.

The course of the day's discussions, however, led me in a different direction. I puzzled over it after they left, examining my own feelings of discomfort over what I perceived as some rather hypocritical statements made. In particular, I thought of the idea of a law, and what it means to break a law.

We broke the law by growing marijuana. This is true. Most people would take the stand that, if the law is broken, there should be a penalty, a price to pay. Some would say that we are paying that price while others will undoubtedly assert, we are "getting off easy" or even getting away with our crime since neither of us is currently sitting in prison.

So, if you break the law, and you are caught, you should pay the price ... right?

Well, let's just leave that question sitting on the table for a moment and I'll ask another now. If there is no victim, is there a crime?

Chew on that for a minute. Don't try to answer it. Just let it sit there on the table right next to the first one.

The evening before, my friend's husband had brought the laptop by for Dave to look at and the conversation had turned to our music collections. Dave was unsure what the guy's stand would be on music that had been downloaded through BitTorrent. My friend's husband just laughed and said, "I have no problem with pirated music and software." He began to list off all of the programs he had gotten for free through file sharing.

Really? Is this the same person who so coolly pointed out to Dave when he griped about the insanity of drug court, "Well, you broke the law, now you have to pay the price."

I've said that this would not be a treatise on why marijuana should be legal or a pity party on how we are being picked on by the judicial system. But that doesn't preclude my sharing my opinion at odd moments, and here is one of them. In our case, I believe that our manufacture of marijuana was a victimless crime. The person we sold it to was an adult, we were adults, and we never exposed our child to the drug or the smell or even the sight of the leafy green stuff.

However, I would postulate that music piracy *does* have a victim – namely the band or individual whose business it is to write, sing, and publish songs (or software or movies or books for that matter). When their hard work is shared for free without their permission, without their making some kind of a profit, then those individuals who download the item are in essence *stealing* from that company, band, or individual. Their crime has a victim, so who is the worst offender?

When the judge compared my husband to a child rapist, she was drawing a direct line from a victimless crime to a crime where there is indisputably a victim, and saying it was the same. I just cannot agree with this premise. Perhaps I'm being an apologist or trying to justify our actions. I'll freely admit that my bias is to see us in the best light possible. But it is food for thought. Think about it and come to your own conclusions.

Day 18 – 8/31/2009
Color: Orange

"Orange! Huh!" Dave set the phone down. "I'm feeling unloved."

I laughed, "Now you, don't you go acting out and making trouble now."

He joked, "I'll go in and make a scene and tell them I'm fiending for the reefer."

"Oh yeah, that's a *great* idea!"

There are many ways we could deal with this situation. We could whine, bitch, blame others, be angry or even depressed … but having a sense of humor about it is usually our default setting. Even if it is gallows humor, it suits us.

It's better than the bad times, those moments when we are both caught in the vortex of frustration. A friend of mine asked, "Did you get my email the other day? I never heard back from you."

I apologized, "I'm sorry I didn't respond. I did get your email, I was just stressing over our situation and alternately feeling sorry for myself or angry at the world."

When I feel those emotions wash over me, I pull away for a few days, deal with them by myself, and then re-emerge and make any necessary apologies. I usually start by reminding myself how it was my bright idea in the first place to do this and that I have no one but myself to blame. When the news first broke, my father was furious with the owners of hydroponics store the police had staked out. It was from there that they had followed Dave after seeing him purchase expensive grow lights. "They could have posted a sign and warned people that the cops were watching," he fumed. I explained that they too had a small child. It wasn't their fault we weren't more careful or more aware of who was watching and it certainly wasn't their fault we had chosen to grow weed with the equipment we purchased from them.

Despite my acceptance and understanding that we had created our situation, there would still be many moments of wishing things were different, wanting the drug court people to just go away, and wishing I had never told another soul about the problems facing us. I hated the air of superiority or condescension we encountered from one couple. In one breath they said, "Well, you broke the law." In the next breath they stated their willingness to download pirated software and music off of the internet. Both acts are against the law, so was our crime worse simply because we got caught?

When I mentioned this to another friend she said, "In for a penny, in for a pound." In other words, it's a crime, either way. Don't do the crime if you aren't willing to pay the price. "Don't speed if you can't afford to pay the ticket," were her words.

And to tell you the truth, I actually agreed with her. Despite her own individual anti-drug stance, she recognized that we were willing to take the hit, learn from it, and move on. It was realistic, down-to-earth support like this that would get me through many hard moments in our journey.

I didn't need someone to say, "Oh honey, they are being so awful, so mean; it's so completely unfair!" It was what it was. And that became my mantra for a very long time. "It is what it is. Now all we can do is get through this."

Dave had been letting his true nature begin to shine through as he tried to forge relationships with the other drug court participants. He has this calming influence, probably from so many years spent practicing the energy arts (Ba Gua, Chi Gung, Tai Chi and more). That morning Anger Management came in and made some snide comment about Dave and Steinbeck being gay since she had seen them practicing martial arts moves.

Dave was slightly annoyed; he looked over and said, "You catch more flies with honey than with sour." And he watched her face crumple. Something was terribly wrong. He pulled her aside and asked her if she was okay. That morning her son had taken a handful of pills after he had left for school. Just a few hours later and they had him in a psychiatric facility.

"It's my fault," she said. When he put a hand on her shoulder, she clutched his hand as if she were drowning. "I'm not coming on to you, but would you please sit next to me in group?" He did as she asked and later, she said, "I don't know what it is about you, but you calm me down."

It is one of Dave's gifts, and as he told me about his day, I wondered how he would fare as a counselor. I think he would be very effective – not just at calming people down, but also by lighting a fire under their ass at just the right moment. His calm encouragement and strong pushes have always felt so perfectly timed when he has helped me through rough patches.

Day 19 – 9/1/2009

Color: Orange and Blue

"Really, hon, you have to hear this guy." Dave put the phone on speaker.

The voice sounded like a bass version of Ben Stein in the 80s classic, *Ferris Bueller's Day Off*, with "You have reached the Cass County Adult Drug program. The color of the day is...orange and blue...orange and blue."

"No love again today."

"Babe, you've been replaced." I think about it for a moment. "Do you guys make jokes about it or what?"

"Oh yeah, I was telling them yesterday that I was having trouble peeing without a man present in the room. I complained that now I have to have my wife come in with me so I can get the job done."

Our lighthearted mood vanished later that morning when the phone rang. "That was Blue Valley," Dave said, seconds later. Blue Valley was a local community center that had agreed to host a Chi Gung class Dave was teaching. "They said that due to a background check they ran on me they were canceling the class."

In my current part-time job, we use an Internet website called Case.net. It shows results for all courts in Missouri – everything from parking tickets to assault, paternity suits to murder. I had recently checked the details on Dave's case and, while it did list the charges, it showed that the case was 'pending disposition.' In other words, due to his participation in the drug court program, it would not show as a conviction. Eventually, when he completed the program successfully it would then register as case dismissed and the records would be sealed. This would not stop any higher-level probe, but on a general level, for a regular, everyday job, it would be more than enough.

I was frustrated, though, at the community center's actions. "It has no final disposition, you are in a diversion program, and they probably think its meth, not weed." Dave just looked sad. It wouldn't have been a lot of money, maybe $40 per week for that one hour early on Wednesday morning. It was the feeling of good it would give him. That he was making *some* money and that he was helping others. "Talk to Sherrie about it, maybe she can do something or suggest something."

He shrugged but agreed that he would mention it in group. Maybe I was hoping for a miracle, or some loophole, I don't know. But anything would be better than just giving up. We left for the day, Dave to Harrisonville, P.E. to daycare, and me to my office job. I shared the frustration of the morning with my friend and she said, "I truly believe that when one door closes another will open. Wait and see; this will turn out well."

After work I ran home, dressed in business casual, got my paperwork, directions and PowerPoint presentation together and left to go teach my "Get Organized, Stay Organized" class to the Mid-Continent Public Library's Blue Springs South location. The class wrapped up at 8:30 but I was delayed at the end of class talking to one of the participants. I drove home, arriving at 9:30 p.m. to an empty house. This was particularly odd. Dave is normally a homebody and now more so because of the requirements of drug court – no leaving the county without permission and a curfew of 10 p.m.

I looked for notes, checked phone messages, tried to find anything that would indicate where he had gone and became progressively frightened as the minutes ticked by. At 9:50 p.m., just ten minutes before his curfew, he drove up in the van with P.E. and he looked scared. "I may be in trouble," he said, "the phone rang at 8:15 and it was the View (a community center in Grandview, just a few minutes from here). They said, 'Mr. Shuck, you have a classroom full of students, where are you?'"

I gasped, "Oh my God, how did we miss putting it on the calendar?" He explained that he had talked to the class coordinator there a few weeks ago and asked her if there was another time that she could schedule the class. At the time he had just received the details of what days he would need to participate in drug court. The class, initially scheduled to start at 4:15 p.m., would simply not be feasible. She had promised to do what she could to move it to a better time, and had done so. She had neglected to tell him about the change since she was in the hospital having a baby!

   When the call had come in from the View, he had packed up P.E. and rushed over there, without even thinking of the fact that he was leaving the county without permission. "Do I tell Sherrie I crossed county lines without permission and go to jail?" he asked, "Or do I see if they catch me?"

   "Call her. Call her now." I advised, hoping desperately that this would not be a repeat of the day he forgotten to call in for the color of the day. If he had to do another shock treatment of 24 hours in jail it would also reset him back to Day One of Phase One and mean another full eight weeks before he could progress to Phase Two. If he didn't call, and it was found out that he had crossed county lines, he would go to jail for 24 hours anyway and it would show he was unwilling to be honest to a fault. Above all, he needed to show complete conformity and acceptance to their rules to progress through the program.

Dave sighed, "I'll call her right now and throw myself on her mercy. Damn it, I really don't want to go to jail. But if I do it now, I'll be out and cleared to teach class on Thursday." I nodded and he disappeared into the other room to make the call. A few minutes later he returned, looking very relieved.

"She said it was work-related and to just call her next time before I left." He managed a smile, "She also said, 'Dave you have got to calm down and go do your Tai Chi before you give yourself a heart attack. You worry too much. And if you want to get those Blue Valley people to give me a call, I will explain to them that you are completely drug-free. Maybe that will encourage them to re-instate your class.'"

A wave of relief washed over me. It was yet another day of ups and down, but it had ended on an 'up' note. Dave was teaching once again and the students had given excellent feedback from the first session. Better yet, he faced no sanctions for straying off the reservation and would continue to be allowed to teach classes in Grandview. We took the small victories where we could find them, held them close, and cherished them. We would get through this, one day at a time.

Day 20 – 9/2/2009
Color: Orange and Green

Dave's day off from drug court, so of course he was required to pee. It was my day off from office work at my friend's and I only had one cleaning to go to. I was going to get a lot of writing done! My fiction book, *War's End: The Storm* was progressing well. I had recently divided the book into two parts, and the first book was just a few chapters away from completion. I would have this day and the next to work on it nearly exclusively. I was, of course, also working on this book you are reading now and Dave worried, not for the first time, how we would be able to publish it. Not surprisingly, he was hyper-sensitive of any possible law-breaking or lawsuit-inducing repercussions.

I finished with my one scheduled cleaning and drove home, all set to get to work. When I arrived, Dave was gone, probably off to submit a UA. As I began to work on *War's End: The Storm* the phone rang, and when I answered a woman asked for Dave. "He's not here right now. He'll probably be back in a half hour or so. Shall I have him call you back?"

The woman was obviously uncomfortable, "Uh yeah, just tell him it's Anger Management. I'm just a friend of his."

"I know; Dave's mentioned you," I tried to sound as friendly and non-threatening as possible.

"I just wouldn't want you to think that I want to start anything, cause I'm not trying to start anything and y'know, he just said I could call if I needed to talk to someone." Slightly circular, and I tried hard not to laugh. She seemed so scared that I would get the wrong impression.

"I know, and it's fine for you to call. I'm okay with it and I'll have him call you back real soon." We said goodbye and I hung up the phone.

I trust my husband. Maybe that is rather Pollyanna of me, but I do. Besides, I know him pretty well. If he wants to make friends with other women, that is fine and acceptable, as long as it stays a friendship. From my experience with him, Dave is a one-woman man, and I didn't think I had anything to worry about. Even if he found her attractive, he would stay true.

A few minutes later, he returned and I relayed the message that she had called. Ten minutes later he came into my office, "She's been cutting herself over this situation with her son." Anger Management's son had taken the new truck out, crashed it, and then tried to overdose on pain meds the next day. He was now in a psych ward and refused to see his family. "She thinks it's all her fault and she says that it feels better to let some of the pressure out." He ran his hands through his hair and shook his head, "How can people get to that point? What's going on in their head that makes cutting themselves and bleeding a viable option?"

    I thought of my ex-boyfriend in California who had told me about how he had started cutting himself in his early 20s. He had been serving with the Coast Guard when his wife took their baby daughter and left him. She had divorced him and gotten complete custody of the baby and he had been miserable and lonely. It all came to a head one day when he was feeling especially stressed. He got into work, plopped down his rucksack, fished out a knife and cut himself, deep, right in front of his co-worker. He didn't even think about it, or how it would look; he just did it. A few hours later and they were committing him to an involuntary psychiatric stay. A few months after that and he was discharged from the Coast Guard.

That was the first time I had heard of people cutting on themselves. It sounded very strange, but mostly it struck me as very sad. How much hate must you have inside you to make your body pay in such a way?

During the call, Dave asked Anger Management, "Are you going to cut again?"

"No. Probably not. Why?"

"Because if you did, I'd have to report it to the counselors."

"If you do that, they'd lock me up for a psych eval!"

"Better that than letting you seriously hurt yourself. I'm your friend and a friend shouldn't let you cut on yourself like that again."

Seeing Dave offer his help to Anger Management, the Hydrocodone addict in NA, and even Steinbeck, reminded me of his anger and frustration in the first week of the program. He had said at one point, "I don't want anything to do with any of these people!" Yet here he was, fielding phone calls, offering support, and even teaching basic martial arts moves to Steinbeck. He was finding a place of calm within the madness, defining his role, and feeling good about himself as he helped others.

I believe that, good or bad, our experiences can help us be better people. It is how we choose to respond to the experiences, what we learn, and how we grow that are important. Dave had said several times that, although he would have preferred *not* to experience drug court or incarceration or any of the legal troubles we have faced, he wanted to take this experience and learn from it. He wanted to look inside himself and see if there were essential truths that he needed to face and learn from. "I can make this a learning experience and take some time for some real introspection," he said. I found that compelling and exciting too. He was growing into a man I respected and appreciated more with each day that passed.

 That afternoon he twisted his ankle hard as he was leaving to go pick up P.E. from daycare. I helped him back inside and went and picked her up myself. After dinner, Dave asked me to drive him to the NA meeting since his ankle was still aching badly. I dropped him off, drove home, and gave P.E. a bubble bath before we drove back to pick him up.

 The night's topic at NA was gratitude. Everyone was encouraged to share a story in which they had felt grateful for something. Dave recounted to me later the story of one man who spoke at the meeting. The man described being released from prison for serving time for drug possession. After his release, he decided to drive to Las Vegas. There he encountered an old friend who he hadn't seen in 30 years. This was a friend from his drug-using days. He told his friend that he was planning on returning to Missouri and the guy asked for a ride. "Just give me a couple of minutes to talk to this guy and I'll be ready to go," he said. When he returned, he was carrying a large duffel bag.

The man learned that his friend had 50 pounds of heroin inside of that bag. When he turned his friend down, explaining that he couldn't risk going back to prison again, his friend called him every name in the book and told him he never wanted to see him again. He stuck to his guns and drove home alone. On his drive back home to Missouri, police pulled his car over twice and after he identified himself as a convicted felon, they searched the car from top to bottom. "I'm so grateful I told my friend 'no' that night. If I hadn't, I would have spent the rest of my life in prison."

Dave then relayed the story of a woman who told of being released from prison and having nothing; no friends, no family, no possessions. She went to an NA meeting on Christmas Day and listened to these people talk about being clean for ten, 20, even 30 years. She felt so sorry for herself that she ran from the room and one of the men followed her. He told her not to give up, and when she told him she could not do it, she wasn't strong enough and she had no will, he took her on a trip. He drove to a nearby hospital and showed her his friend who, after getting so high that he drove his car into a tree, ended up losing both his legs and so much blood that he suffered a catastrophic stroke and was a vegetable.

    The last story he told me was the hardest to hear. Shark told a story of her friend, a young man who had been drinking and got behind the wheel, driving drunk on a sunny Saturday afternoon. He went off the road, hit a young mother and her baby as she was walking and pushing the stroller. He killed them instantly and ended his catastrophic journey by driving partly into someone's house. Shark described him as being a real nice guy, friendly, outgoing, very gregarious. After the accident, she visited him in jail and said that his eyes looked dead. He refused the legal counsel his parents tried to hire for him and told the judge, "Give me the maximum. Put me away for life. I hope I live to be 100, and spend every minute of it inside prison. I will remember every hour of every day what I did. I wish you could kill me the same way in which they died. That's the only justice I deserve."

I could hear the raw pain in Dave's voice as he repeated these stories to me. "These people have had so much pain, so much heartache. I can't even imagine what their lives have been like and how they have managed to survive."

He had asked a man in the Belton NA meeting the week before to be his sponsor and the man turned him down. The man did not feel he was far enough along in the process to be that person that would make a good sponsor. Dave said, "If I had been turned down like that before, I would have cracked open a beer and rolled a big fat joint. It was hard getting turned down." He told the NA members the same thing that night. "I'm grateful for NA and drug court for taking away that alternative, so that I could learn how to deal with my bruised pride without the help of drugs."

When he said that, I could not help but ask, "Do you really mean that? Or were you just saying it to say it there and gain acceptance?"

"I really meant it."

For the first time in years, I began to wonder if I had been a co-dependent. Was I helping to maintain status quo? Was I encouraging my husband to self-medicate instead of helping him work through rejection or failure or other difficulties?

These questions bothered me. I did not want to be a co-dependent or an enabler. I wanted a healthy, happy relationship with my husband. One built on respect, strength, and love. I believed that we had that, but still these questions were not easily dismissed or swept under the rug. I had to answer them – for myself, for my husband, and for our child.

Day 22 – 9/4/2009
Color: Orange and Yellow

Court day. Dave didn't say it, but I knew he was nervous. The judge had terrified him the week before and he asked me to iron his shirt and pants so that he looked as presentable as possible. I wondered if she would apologize to him for her mistake. Highly unlikely, but still, I hoped. I have always preferred to believe in the innate good in people, no matter what their position or station in life. I didn't want to feel like this process was 'us' against 'them.' In some ways I hoped that a partnership, however unequal, would form.

Whoever dreamed up this program did it for a reason and I didn't believe it was just to keep people out of prison. I believed, or really wanted to believe, that the program's founder(s) wanted to help people, to access their humanity, to tear away the bad habits, and create new and better ones. It may have become a distortion of the dream, but still, what can you expect? Humans made the program to help other humans and both sides have plenty of flaws. No matter what dream you have, or vision of what you want to accomplish, reality alters it. People indulge in power plays and snipe and manipulate. This is true of everyone, no matter how kind or good they are. We seek to control our world; that's human nature.

    The fate of Pit Bull would also be decided on this day. In the first days of the program she had been put into jail. She continued to claim that her husband had given her the Tramadol for a headache and that she hadn't known what it was until later. Her story unraveled when her husband did not verify her claim. It would turn out that she had been stealing money from friends and family and using it to buy prescription drugs using forged doctor's prescriptions. This, along with the alarming news that she had also been having sex with a teenage neighbor in exchange for other prescription drugs, brought on a showdown in the courtroom two weeks prior.

Her husband had confessed to her that he had also been sleeping around, with three of her closest friends. With friends like that, who needs enemies? He also intended to file for divorce and leave the state with their two children, ensuring she would never see them again.

She reacted so badly to this news that they put her on suicide watch. In the Cass County jail this meant an isolation cell and the dreaded "turtle suit." Designed to confine and protect, the turtle suit was a padded suit with a hood. The prisoner is zippered inside and their wrists handcuffed in front of them. It is impossible to use the toilet without help from the jailer. This meant that each time she needed to use the facilities she had to ask for a female officer to come and help her.

Throw into this mix that you are also not allowed underwear in isolation, and for part of the week she had been having her period. The turtle suit was loose, so she had to grip the pad between her legs and then call for a female officer when she needed to change that as well. Pit Bull was allowed to leave the jail and wear regular clothes during the day as she attended the group meetings, but she was terrified of what the judge would do to her.

She was given a 120-day shock time. That meant 120 days in jail and, if she maintained exemplary behavior, she could then return to the program as a Phase One at Day 1. In other words, it would be nearly two more years. Add to this the twist that, when she was released after her 120 days in jail, she could not return home. She would have to find alternate housing, and not be able to see her children, possibly for up to two years.

This sobered me, just the thought of not being able to see your children or raise them or be in their lives. This is what drugs had done to this woman. She had placed getting high and feeling good over being a mother to her children. And I wondered, not for the first time, how a person's priorities can get so messed up. It is a question that continues to haunt me.

Dave's turn came in front of the judge. He approached the bench and the judge said, "Mr. Shuck."

"Yes, your honor."

"Guess what we *aren't* going to do today?"

"I, uh, I don't know, your honor."

"We aren't going to engage in a theoretical political debate today."

"Thank you, your honor." And he meant it, quite sincerely.

"I see you have been doing well in the program, Mr. Shuck, and that you are currently seeking a sponsor."

"Yes, your honor."

"And how many days now, Mr. Shuck?" She was referring to the number of days both alcohol and drug free. Dave had stopped smoking at the end of November 2008, but his last beer had been on July 21st, 2009. His sobriety was counted from the last beer, *not* the last time he had smoked marijuana

"Forty days, your honor."

"You may sit down now, Mr. Shuck."

"Thank you, your honor."

As others had told us, there was no apology from the judge, no admitting failure of any kind. I hadn't expected it, but I had certainly hoped for it. She did at least acknowledge that Dave was doing well, and I grasped at this and felt I would have to be content. However, her refusal to admit a mistake sent one message loud and clear, "Do as I say, not as I do." With directives like that to follow, is it any surprise that lying and deceit and mistrust on both sides flourish?

Many of the Phase Four participants were at Friday court. They eyed Dave's dress shirt, pants, and tie and sneered quietly until they were out of the courtroom. Most of the Phase

Four's wore jeans and T-shirts. They accused him of being a kiss-ass.

"This is court. When I go to court, I will dress appropriately," Dave explained to them.

"I wouldn't be caught dead wearing a suit all day long," said one.

"That's why I bring a change of clothes."

"Whatever."

A neighbor's brother, who is a meth addict, was also in court that day. The judge took her time with him. He was a Phase Three, but he had had setbacks in the past. Namely, he had gotten caught, by the judge herself, after he returned home from a bar, drunk. She had sat in his driveway, waiting 45 minutes, until he returned past his curfew and in violation of drug court rules. She drove him down to Harrisonville herself and checked him into the jail.

As a result of that and a few other bumps along the way, he had been in the program for over two years now. After she ran down the list of his failures along the way, and reminded him that if he had just kept his nose clean, he would have been out by now, she elevated him to a Phase Four. This is the final level of the program and usually lasts a minimum of five months. If he was incredibly well-behaved, he might even complete it, and consequently the full drug court program, in just three more months.

After just three weeks, I had come to view court day more as circus day. The freaks and the stories...how they all come out of the woodwork! Just like the show *Weeds*, Friday court is the gory, mashed-up accident on the highway that draws my attention and sucks me in.

Next up was Casanova, who had slept with several of the drug court participants, also a big no-no and listed as a terminating offense.

Casanova had been instructed to write a letter to the court explaining why sleeping with other drug court participants was a bad idea. He was then required to read it out loud that day. Now when you consider the level of literacy of the average drug court participant, this was a painful exercise to listen to. But if that wasn't enough to cow him and bring him back into line, the judge also brought up the fact that Casanova has a live-in girlfriend. She informed him that she was going to talk to the girlfriend and gave him the option of explaining things to the girlfriend first. "I think you had better explain to your girlfriend the details before I do, Mr. Casanova."

"Yes, ma'am."

After court Dave attended the diversion program. One of the other attendees, actually not a drug court participant but there as part of CSTAR*, was Anger Management. Another drug court participant, Shark, had overheard him telling Anger Management that she could call him any time she needed someone to talk to. Shark is a Phase Four and a favorite of the judge. "You need to worry about your own sobriety right now," she admonished Dave.

The Friday before, Shark had been brought in by the judge to unleash on Pit Bull. Apparently, Shark had been her mentor/sponsor. After she had finished ripping Pit Bull up, she had walked up to Dave, as he sat shaking from his encounter with the judge, and asked, "What did you do to piss off the judge?" When he replied that he hadn't done anything, she turned up her nose, "You are a liar. I don't waste my time with liars."

After court, Anger Management came up to Dave and asked him if he could give her a lift to the NA meeting that night. "I'm sorry, I can't, and there are two reasons why. First, I'm going to a wedding tonight. And second, you are still smoking marijuana, and I can't endanger my own recovery or place in drug court by exposing myself to possible arrest if you are caught in my car with drugs on you."

Dave nearly jumped out of his skin when Shark materialized at his side. She had been standing there listening to the entire conversation. "Wow," she stared at him, "I am really impressed. That was just so right on and focused of you. You explained why and you had obviously thought it through." Considering that one week ago Shark was convinced he was a liar that was high praise indeed.

The rest of the day passed uneventfully. Dave had made special arrangements to leave the county to attend his cousin's wedding and the counselors allowed him to leave at 2:45 instead of 4 p.m. I had arranged to work until 3:30. The wedding was at 5 p.m. and at least 45-minute drive away, so we didn't have a lot of time. We dressed and left by 4pm. We soon found ourselves stuck in a mess of construction, rain and rush-hour traffic. By the time we had made it about a mile from our destination it was five minutes past 5:00. And the location? Well, we couldn't seem to find it.

I finally broke down and called his aunt. "We can't seem to find the event." I said.

"That would be because it's not for another three weeks."

"Oh, yeah, that would do it." I said goodbye and started laughing. All the damned traffic we had waded through, not to mention the special permissions and how we had taken off early from work and drug court, and I had never once looked at the invitation.

I would later swear that Dave had told me the 5th and he would swear that he had never said that or looked at the invitation himself. We returned, crept through even worse traffic on the return trip, and finally made it back to Belton. "I'm starving; take me to Backyard Burger now or your life will be forfeit," I demanded.

"Yes, dear."

As if I hadn't had enough fun in the car already, as we pulled out of the drive thru, I suggested, "You might as well just head down to Harrisonville to drop a UA there." Any time he is allowed out of Cass County, except for teaching his Chi Gung classes, he must submit a UA at the County Sheriff's office upon his return. We turned onto the highway and headed south. Twenty minutes later, just a few miles out of Harrisonville, the traffic stopped. Everyone was trying to get out of town for the long Labor Day weekend.

We just looked at each other for the umpteenth time and laughed. It was either laugh, scream, or cry, and I guess we both figured it was easier to laugh. P.E. practically levitated out of her chair when we stopped at the jail. "I have to pee!" Right kid, of course you do.

We made a sight, I'm sure. All three of us dressed up, P.E. in her "Jackie O" dress and me in a nice dress and sandals, walking into a jail so that my husband could drop a UA and my little one could use the facilities. We were watched on the cameras the entire time. I finished helping P.E. and we walked back out to the van to wait for Dave. A few minutes later, P.E. announced, "I have to poop!"

"Oh no. No, no, no, no, NO." There was no way I was going back inside that jail. It might nominate me for the bad mother of the year award, but I couldn't bear going back in there, "Child, you are just going to have to hold it." And hold it she did. She held it for the ten minutes it took for Dave to return, and the 20 minutes more it took for us to return to Belton. All in all, we had been in that car for four hours!

That night, at precisely 12:15 a.m., the doorbell rang. I grabbed Dixie, our little dog with a loud bark, and put her outside. Dave let Officer Wheatfield in and I went back to bed.

Day 23 - 9/5/2009
Color: Orange and Yellow and later, Blue

They didn't change the colors over from the day before until 7:45 a.m. After Day 3, Dave made it a priority to call in first thing in the morning. This usually meant 7:15 at the latest. Since the call must be made from your home phone, there is a call log; the drug court always knows exactly when a participant called. No matter what, since his color was green, he didn't need to submit a UA. But he did learn that the old color from the day before applied to those who were listed as calling in before the changeover. For those who called after 7:45, the color blue applied. It was good to know that this area would not serve as a trap – one in which they would tell him, "You should have called in twice, just to make sure."

Dave recounted his day as he cooked stir fry chicken and vegetables for dinner. He had begun to take on a leadership role in the group meetings. Most of that day's group had focused on Steinbeck, the young guy who had spit out the phlegm and left it on the courtroom floor. Not known for his mental prowess, he was regularly denigrated by the other drug court participants. Dave had been showing him martial arts moves and taken Steinbeck under his wing.

"We focused on how Steinbeck needs to make better choices and avoid people who will get him into trouble," Dave said as the chicken sizzled in the pan. "Taking his sister up on an invitation to go swimming included trespassing, everyone including him drinking beer, and the cops being called. And all of this happened while he was in drug court!" He shook his head. "The sister is openly contemptuous of drug court, so she's continuing to try to get him in bad situations and he still wants to hang out with her."

Three weeks into the program and he was definitely forming attachments to his fellow participants. Human beings are social creatures, and I believe it is difficult to stop yourself from forming at least some attachment to individuals you see day in and day out. I doubt there was a single individual in there that we would have normally felt comfortable with, or invited over to our house for dinner or socializing. But Dave was fitting in, and growing, and doing his best. I was proud of him; he was stepping up and adding his expertise in martial arts and even common good sense to help others, and consequently himself, through a difficult process.

Shortly before dinner was finished, my mother showed up to pick up her computer. A virus had shut it down and Dave had spent a day reloading it. She stayed for dinner and then after P.E. woke up, she took her home with her to spend the night. I sent them home in the van so we wouldn't need to fuss with changing out the car seat and promised to come by the next day and pick her up. I also needed to dig up the daylilies I had been promising to take from her.

That night, when I was well and thoroughly asleep and Dave was watching *Matrix Revolutions* on our bedroom television, the doorbell rang again. This time it was Deputy Good Ole Boy. Dave told me to go back to bed and I did. The visits from the trackers were becoming routine for us and he had gotten breathing into the Breathalyzer and submitting a urine sample down to a science. In less than five minutes, the tracker was on his way to another house. This was the first time we had seen trackers at our door two nights in a row but I was not surprised. It was a three-day weekend, with Monday being Labor Day. The last hurrah of summer meant parties, visiting the lake and drinking beer. They were keeping a close eye on all of us.

Despite the warnings that they would go through our house with a fine-toothed comb, I doubt anyone had ever envisioned our house when saying that. It's filled with so many nooks and crannies that there is no way a tracker would find something if we chose to hide it. It would take hours and hours of looking and the program simply didn't have the manpower for that.

Not that I would risk it, because I wouldn't. It was not worth risking Dave's liberty or his ability to stay here in the house with us while he completed the program. As it was, when our big dog Kellogg developed her seasonal allergies, we even called Sherrie to tell her that there would be Benadryl in the house for the dog. We fed her four tablets a day to reduce her itching and hair loss. Meanwhile, Dave was also affected by allergies, mainly to the ragweed which was in full bloom. He had to suffer through it with only Tylenol and Excedrin for the massive headaches.

If and when I got a cold, I would ask Dave to call Sherrie and inform her that we would like to have Nyquil on the premises. Due to the high alcohol content, Nyquil, like mouthwash, was banned. The idea of some poor SOB actually drinking that stuff to get drunk freaked me out. How low did one have to get before doing that seemed a viable option?

Day 25 – 9/7/2009
Color: Yellow
One of the requirements of drug court is that Dave must attend three Narcotics

Anonymous meetings per week. We had worked out a schedule of Monday, Wednesday, and Friday for this once he began teaching Chi Gung classes on Tuesday and Thursday nights. However, he had missed the Friday meeting during our four miserable hours in the car searching for the wedding that wasn't going to be held for another three weeks, and needed to make it up so that he still had three for the week. He found one that was being held at noon and he also planned to attend his regular Monday evening meeting. Two meetings in one day would put him back on schedule and show that he was conforming to the expectations of drug court.

 He hadn't looked at the schedule of meetings closely, and found himself, at noon, in an Alcoholics Anonymous meeting instead of Narcotics Anonymous. One of the guys in the meeting gave him a heads up before everything got started, "When you introduce yourself, don't just say your name and that you are an addict," he advised. "Tell them you are an alcoholic and a drug addict. They're a bit sensitive about the difference."

 I found that interesting that there would be a distinction. Did alcoholics truly believe that alcohol was not a drug? Or that someone could be an alcoholic, but that didn't make them a drug addict? To me it seemed a bit like splitting hairs. Apples or oranges, they are, after all, still fruit. It reminded me of 12 years before when I had first moved here with Danielle and moved in with my mother. "Go to the store for me," my mother had asked, "and buy me a pack of cigarettes."

"I'm not buying your drugs for you," I'd said.

"They're not drugs!" She'd been incensed at the idea that I viewed smoking cigarettes the same as illicit drugs.

It made me wonder. What is the definition of a drug? I looked it up in several places.

According to Wikipedia – "A drug, broadly speaking, is any substance that, when absorbed into the body of a living organism, alters normal bodily function."

Well, if we use that description, even chocolate or coffee would be considered a drug, not just alcohol or tobacco. In fact, that same article in Wikipedia has a picture of a cup of coffee with a caption that reads, "Coffee is the most widely used psychotropic beverage in the world."

However, the *Compact Oxford English Dictionary* sitting on my desk reads, "an illegal substance taken for its narcotic or stimulant effects." Huh. Okay, definitely not alcohol, coffee, chocolate, or cigarettes in that category.

And finally, Dictionary.com weighs in by defining the word drug as, "any article, other than food, intended to affect the structure or any function of the body of humans or other animals." Now my brain was really getting mixed up. Is coffee considered a *food*? What about psychedelic mushrooms? Do they count as food?

The others in the AA meeting gave Dave the phone list and urged him to call, "Remember, you will fail; we all do. The important thing is to keep trying and eventually you will get there." Over and over, throughout the drug court and the meetings and even the officials that same message continued to be repeated, "*You will fail. You will fail* because you are a hopeless addict."

If failure meant ever drinking or using drugs again, then yes, that would be true. Dave had no intention of never using drugs again or never drinking beer again. But stopping for a year and a half while he made it through drug court and his record was wiped clean? That was unquestioned. I didn't lose one night's sleep over it, or worry that Dave would be sneaking a nip off the Nyquil or guzzling mouthwash. And there was no way he was going to risk spending another night in jail just for the taste of a beer.

Again, I found myself questioning the very nature of addiction. Who is an addict? What does that person look like, act like, and how do they live? Is there such a thing as use without abuse?

Were we being short-sighted or simply not understanding what addiction was? Could we possibly fit into some strange, uncharted territory or category where there was neither addiction nor abuse?

As Dave recounted the AA meeting to me, he stopped and said, "I'm learning from all of this. I really am. But I don't believe I'm an alcoholic and I don't believe I'm a drug addict. Yes, I have abused drugs, and yes, at times I've probably drank more than I should, but in neither case do I feel I am an addict."

And I had to agree. I didn't see the addiction either, not at all. And again, I found myself wondering, *does that make me a co-dependent?* How else could I explain how my view and opinion could directly contradict the professional opinion of the court and so many of the other experts?

Day 27 – 9/9/2009
Color: Green and all Level Four
"Wow. It's been what, a week?"

"Yep." It had actually been six days since his color came up.

"Well, damn. I guess I shouldn't have smoked all that pot."

He was joking, obviously. Danielle's plane had been an hour late and it had been another full hour before we returned home. I had been exhausted and had gone to bed at 11 p.m. while Dave and Danielle stayed up and talked and listened to music until midnight.

Dave had an hour to make up with drug court after taking off early one day the previous week. I had two cleanings to get done that day. They were relatively small cleanings, and I returned by 1 p.m. to an empty house. A few minutes later, Danielle and Dave returned with groceries.

We put groceries away and I wandered back to my office with Danielle close behind. She sat down and said, "I'm seriously considering moving back to Missouri." She had just broken up with her boyfriend and would be returning to a one-bedroom apartment that she couldn't afford to pay for on her own.

We talked about her options and I offered to drive out in my minivan, pick her and her belongings up, and then drive back. Later that evening she suggested she could fly out on a one-way ticket and help me drive out there as well. We drew up a tentative budget and looked at plane fares. She had to wait until the end of December, when the one-year lease was up, before she could return. That meant nearly four months alone in the apartment, but her boyfriend had paid up his half of the rent through the end of the year and told her he would move out the week she was gone in Missouri.

In some ways I think that made it a bit easier for her, not to see his things being taken from the apartment. But the emptiness of the apartment and his absence would also be a hard thing to return to. This had been her first serious relationship as an adult living on her own. And the decision to move in together had been a big one for both of them.

That evening she looked at me and asked, "Mom, were you serious when you offered to drive all the way out to California to get me?" I looked in her face and remembered how many times I had put my life and my dreams and my education on hold for this girl. I thought about the years of worrying, loving, and tears. I remembered the moments when we had fought, and many more moments when we had not. I could still hear her confession from earlier in the day ringing in my ears, "When you and I fought and I left home, I blamed you. I blamed you for two years. Everything was your fault. I know now that was wrong. I think I knew it even then."

Even at 21, she was still my child. I could take a week out of my life and give it to her easily. I had certainly done far more for her in the years before. "Yes, Danielle. I will do this for you. It won't be easy; it's a hell of a lot of driving, 1,500 miles each way. But yes, I do mean it and I will do it."

My elation that evening at having my firstborn back in the same area near me was dimmed only by Dave's lack of excitement. He was tight-lipped about it that evening. As we lay in bed, I asked him what was going on. He was guarded in his response, choosing his words carefully.

"I don't know how I will feel about staying here once this is all done."

"Are you worried that if Danielle is here, I won't want to leave?" I asked.

"I don't know what you'll want to do."

"Honestly honey, I don't either. We don't know what will happen or whether moving back to California would be any better than a change of scenery." I said, "What if we move back and there are no jobs there either? I have nightmares about all three of us ending up living in the front room of your parents' house! How will walking away from what we have here change anything?"

He was silent, so I continued, "All I'm worried about right now is surviving all of this. So, I will continue to work at the office, run the cleaning biz, teach the classes, and concentrate on getting my books out and published. Right now, that's what I need to do. Eventually we will move back to California. But when that will be is really up in the air right now. Until we get through this, that's where it needs to stay."

He agreed and the conversation shifted to that evening's NA meeting. "I don't know if I feel comfortable including any of the details of the NA meetings in the book."

I asked him why and he said, "Because it's anonymous, and some of these people," he paused, "their stories are so difficult to listen to. Christine, they come back every week, every few days even, even when they don't have to."

I could hear the emotion in his voice, "They aren't required to do it. The court doesn't force them to go to meetings and yet they show up. Every week."

I understood this. He felt protective of these people and in awe of their willingness to lay their souls bare. He had seen how difficult their lives had become as a result of their addiction.

You cannot participate in a program this intensive, and this invasive and not be affected in some way. Dave was slowly being altered in his ways of thinking. So was I, despite being relegated to the sidelines. Our resistance to the program had melted somewhat. It had begun to change in strange and mysterious ways. And while it was still an experience "to just get through" it was now also a vehicle for introspection. How were our lives affected by the use of drugs and alcohol? What parts worked or worked against us when we allowed those substances into our life?

I had begun to realize the full impact of the story I was writing. This had never been a thumb your nose at the man account of how we escaped serving hard time for our crimes. But I had begun it far more light-hearted than it deserved. I found myself struggling with definitions and meanings. I wanted to understand the very nature of addiction and how it affected not just us, but these other people. What did it mean to be an alcoholic? When did use become abuse? When did it become addiction?

These questions continued to swirl through my head each day. The path ahead was rocky and dimly lit. Which way would it turn next?

Day 29 – 9/11/2009
Color: Green

The Friday began with a record morning for drug court. Each Phase One participant met with the judge, there was no drama or excitement and within seven minutes of the start of court, everything was done and complete. The judge asked Dave about how the visit with Danielle was going and inquired into his success in finding an NA sponsor. "I'm still looking, your honor," was all that Dave could tell her.

That evening he had success. The second person he asked said, "yes" and he was extremely excited. "We meet tomorrow to discuss it," he smiled, "This is one of three steps I need to complete to graduate to Phase Two. I also need to complete part of a workbook which I've finished about half of, and the third thing," he looked embarrassed. "I've forgotten what the third thing is."

No matter; he would get a handle on that by Monday at the latest.

Part of the drug court program includes community service and he was approached by a counselor and told that he had been tapped to serve one of the upcoming weekend days. The counselor asked if Dave wanted to do it Saturday or Sunday and Dave jumped at the opportunity to do it on Saturday, which still counted as his required time at the counseling center in Harrisonville. This meant that Sunday would remain open for all of us to do something together, with Danielle, as a family.

That evening, while Danielle was out visiting with friends, a tracker came. He was new, not the other two we had seen before. Dave had heard reports that during the long weekend prior, several participants' houses had been searched thoroughly. He had expected he would be next, and asked if the officer needed to see any areas of the house. The man said "no" and asked Dave a few questions, administered a Breathalyzer, and within a few minutes was on to the next house.

Day 30 - 9/12/2009
Color: Green and Level Four

"Where is your community service at?" I asked Dave.

"In Peculiar, at the recycling center," he was dressed in an old T-shirt and jeans. "Mr. Big got a sanction there the other day."

I raised my eyebrows. Mr. Big was a tall, black, ex-crack cocaine dealer. "Oh, really?"

"Someone told him to dig into this smelly container full of rank crap and he refused. She got in his face, called him a 'damn druggie' or something along those lines, and he lost his cool and said, 'Fuck off, bitch.'"

I winced, "Ouch, well that would do it."

"He was almost thrown out of the program because that was his eleventh or twelfth sanction."

Mr. Big had been in the program for nearly two years. Just a year before, he had left county without permission to give his nephew a ride. As he drove through a seedier section of Kansas City, he had been recognized by some rival drug dealers. They had approached the vehicle and shot inside it several times, hitting his nephew in the head and chest. His nephew had died in his arms.

Just a week or so before had been the one-year anniversary and Mr. Big was hurting pretty bad. Having the run-in with the woman at the recycling center had not helped matters. They had stopped short of throwing Mr. Big out of the program after the woman's reluctant admission that she "may have said something inappropriate to him."

Immediately I worried about Dave. Not that he would react as Mr. Big had done, but that he might be asked to do things that were demeaning by someone who had a predetermined mindset on who he was because of where he was. This concerned me.

Being in the program is a hit to your feelings of self-worth, of your competency, and of your existence as an equal member of society. People can look down on you, put you in a neat little box labeled addict, dust off their hands, and walk away. God knows, we had felt that way about his fellow participants in the beginning. It's easy to do. Human nature urges us to define our world – good, bad, right, wrong – to the point that we lose ourselves in general images and labels.

We forget how unique we really are.

I had encountered this to my dismay, in the first week of the program. My father, an ex-pat living in South America, wrote the following:

"When they come in and bust Dave for something ridiculous like a bottle of vanilla extract try and keep your temper in check. I know how you can be, and if you aren't careful you will get Dave hauled off to jail."

Nice. Thanks Dad.

I responded, "Thanks for pigeon-holing me…" to which he replied, "You're welcome." I shut down the secure connection we had been corresponding on and made myself unavailable through any of the encrypted chats he had insisted I install on my computer. His paranoia about someone listening in to our open emails or phone calls would prevent him from contacting me through the normal channels.

A small, petty part of me smiled inside, knowing he would be curious as to how things were going and frustrated at not being updated. His birthday was September 19th. I was not looking forward to calling him, but I would. I'm an only child and I do try and be somewhat polite or thoughtful in regard to special days like birthdays and holidays. It would be the first time we had spoken in weeks.

I had been incredibly offended by his comments. Why did I consider them offensive? For two reasons:

1. Despite the years that had passed, he still seemed to view me as a 16-year-old with no control over my temper. He was also quite oblivious to the fact that it took enormous patience to deal with him or my mother at times. In fact, others had noticed my patience in the face of some rather extreme behavior on both of their parts in the past and asked me how I managed to keep my cool. In spite of all of my patience and efforts to be patient and understanding of their quirks, it was obvious that the label

remained. In my father's eyes I was still 16 years old and too dumb to know when to shut my mouth.

    2. Despite the situation, not everyone in the drug court was out to get us. Many of them wanted us to succeed. When Officer Wheatfield had pointed to the Nyquil, despite Dave's probation officer Sherrie noting that it was okay to have in the house (as long as Dave didn't imbibe), we had poured it out in front of him and that had been more than acceptable. The same had occurred with mouthwash. To date, no one had insisted on going through our spice cabinet, and I doubted that vanilla extract (which does contain alcohol) would be considered a problem.

I regretted telling my father about our situation, but I had hoped for legal advice in those first few days. Once upon a time he had practiced law in Missouri and in Arizona, but it had been a long time since. My mother still did not know, and I planned on keeping it that way for as long as possible. If my dad was any indication of how much worry and interference I would need to deal with in addition to my own, my mother would be ten times worse. She could make a career out of worrying about others.

I thought again of how easy it is to pigeonhole others into a nice, neat category. The woman at the recycling center who referred to the drug court participants as "you druggies" or my mother who had far too many racist and biased views for me to repeat here, or my dad's paranoia about any and all things government – all of these people had limited thinking, and narrowed understanding of the capabilities of those they had categorized and labeled.

I knew we would see more of it in the weeks and months to come. It bothered me and popped out in weird and sudden ways, like on Facebook the day before, when I posted a scathing comment about "small minds and smaller hearts" on a high school classmate's post and then immediately defriended him.

We had been casual friends in high school. He had been very different and we had no shared interests. But sometimes he had been fun, we had been on the fringes of one of the outcast groups, and we had kept in touch over the years after graduating. He had been turned down for just about every fire department or law enforcement job he had applied for and I was certain it was the psych exams that he failed. He had always seemed a bit off in high school, full of anger, and had hinted at a difficult home life.

Years after high school he had converted to the Mormon faith, he met a girl who had done the same, and they had married and had children. Dave and I had thought that his conversion and subsequent marriage had seemed to settle him, to clear out the massive well of anger and rage that he had shown only hints of during our school years together, but as the years progressed it had turned into a judgmental holier-than-thou attitude, I found offensive. We had settled into a rhythm of exchanging annual newsletters about our families at Christmas-time and that was about it until he made an appearance on Facebook a few months before.

He had been carping on Obama's speech to school children and I couldn't stand to listen to his thinly-disguised racist views or self-righteous vomit any longer. The day before I had posted the comment, hit the Cancel button on my friend list to de-friend him, and drove home with a pounding headache and upset stomach.

I believed that I was experiencing a major turning point in my own acceptance of other's personality quirks. I was finding myself less and less willing to tolerate hypocritical viewpoints. Also, when I encountered viewpoints that were, in my view, extremely at odds with my own, I had almost no patience or willingness to deal with them.

    I feared that though. I wanted to keep an open mind, to see other's points of view and understand them as best I could. I didn't want to close myself off to all other ways of thinking, because I believed that doing so was what led so many others to the close-minded (i.e., lack of) thinking they had now. I didn't like or want the "us against them," or the "it's either black or white" mentality. It was a struggle from within that would continue to haunt me that day and long afterwards.

    Danielle had returned at some point in the early morning hours and was asleep on the couch, snuggled against a large stuffed dog of P.E.'s and partially wrapped in the quilt I had made for her. I wanted to wake her up, but I knew she probably had gotten in late from visiting friends. I hoped she would wake up and we could go to Powell Gardens and walk through the grounds and see the new additions to the park. I had heard of a new section, a quilt of food that had been planted and was dying to see it. Either that or a visit to the museum on Main Street in Belton or the old cemetery to see if we could find Carry Nation's grave. I had realized recently, that after 11 years of living in Belton I had still not visited these places. Danielle loved history as much as I did, and I knew she would be up for some adventuring once she had rested.

In the end, we did very little that day, settling instead for a walk with P.E. and one of the dogs. After Dave returned from his day of volunteer work and group therapy, he filled us in on the events of the day while Danielle prepared veggie spring rolls for dinner.

The recycling center was near a school and there was ACT testing scheduled for that day. Dave and another man were in charge of heading off the cars full of stressed-out teenagers, directing them to park in a location farther away. Worried about being late, frustrated that they couldn't park near the school, and general test anxiety led one boy to shout at Dave's partner, "I should kick your ass, old man, but I gotta take a test."

Old Man called out to him, "I'll be here when you get out." He looked over at Dave and shrugged, "I was in the Navy, and I'd like to think I'd give him a run for his money."

My fears of irrational or megalomaniacal recycling center supervisors were unfounded. The only other interesting occurrence of the day was a woman who drove up with a load of rotting, stinking garbage and insisted, "There's paper in there to be recycled."

When she was turned away, rotting meat thick and heavy in the air, she yelled, "I won't bother coming here again." The other workers looked relieved at that promise.

After four hours of community service Dave grabbed a sandwich and drove to group in Harrisonville. Since Saturday group is only for Level One participants, and others were serving community service that weekend as well, there were only three others at group that day, Beer Brat, Casanova and Little Girl.

Little Girl was brand new to the drug court program. She had celebrated her 20th birthday just a week or two before and was struggling daily with her addiction to crystal meth. The sight of a discarded spoon on the lunch table had triggered her just a few days before and she was on edge as they sat out on a smoke break.

Casanova was admiring his new muscles. He had been working out with weights rather obsessively over the past few weeks and the veins in his muscles stood out as he flexed them over and over.

Little Girl had abused meth for years, nearly eight of them, and had usually injected the drugs intravenously. As Casanova flexed his muscles, making his veins protrude from the surface of his muscled arms, Little Girl began to twitch nervously. She turned away from Casanova after her pleas for him to stop were ignored. The veins were a trigger for her, and she was craving drugs and trying to keep control. Dave watched her, uncomprehending of the situation until it escalated way too far. Accidental blows from her, then a forceful return shove by Casanova, and anger and tears. Casanova stalked off, got in his car and drove away. He was finished with his hours for the day, but the others still had a couple more to go.

Despite Little Girl's claims that she was fine, Dave had been rather upset by the entire incident and brought it up in group after break was over. After hearing what happened, Sonia, the counselor leading the meeting, called Casanova and ordered him back to group. He was defensive, and both Little Girl and Casanova were rather unhappy with Dave. The next day they were scheduled to volunteer together at the local recycling center, and Dave came home that evening concerned that the next day would be full of tension and possibly escalate into blows again.

Day 31 – 9/13/2009
Color: Orange and Level Four
It was Sunday and both Dave and P.E. seemed to be getting sick. No work on the

chicken coop, and no planned activities. When I asked Danielle if she wanted to go out, she said, "Honestly Mom, when I was planning for the visit, I was thinking of lots of things I wanted to do. But now that I'm here, and I'm sure I want to move back, it just feels nice spending time with all of you. We don't have to do anything."

Each day of the visit we had talked of the idea more and more. She didn't want her old room back, which was currently my office. That worked for me; I wasn't really ready to give it up! After I had put P.E. down for a nap we had gone down into the basement and talked over the possibilities in that area. There was Ground Zero, the former marijuana room which was now filled with boxes and very, very dark. The task force had taken all of the light sources during their raid!

I located a lamp, plugged it in, and suggested we take the hidden door off of its hinges and put the futon bed inside with a bedside table and lamp. That would leave my craft room intact at one end of the basement and the middle part free for a living/writing and working space for Danielle.

Our use of the basement was minimal. The laundry room was down there and plenty of storage was open in the crawl spaces. I hoped to keep my craft room, which was nestled at the far end of the basement. Now that P.E. was older, I was actually able to come down and sew on quilts and had some organizing to do to get the room in shape.

Danielle thought the old marijuana room was a bit creepy, less so once we put in a light, and she offered to help finish out the ceiling with drywall like the rest of the basement. "Mom if you don't get around to cleaning up down here before I arrive, don't worry about it. I know you are busy and you have a life. I can always sleep on the couch for a few nights if I need to."

We still didn't know if she would even be allowed to move back into the house. The only situation of its kind that Dave had heard of had been of a father moving back into his son's house. The father was an alcoholic and the court advised the son, who was a drug court participant, that if his father continued to drink, they would leave him there and put the son in jail until he could find better living arrangements.

Danielle occasionally drank and on very rare occasions indulged in smoking weed. Her opinions of weed were about the same as mine. She was also a writer and an artist and didn't particularly like the effect it had on her art. She also knew what was at stake and had volunteered to stop smoking weed and submit to any drug or alcohol tests the court required in order to move in. I looked at her and realized she was actually willing to conform to the court's proscribed rules and lifestyle, just so she could live with us. For some reason I found that fascinating. She wasn't busy trying to figure out ways around the rules, she understood all too well, and she was willing to make sacrifices in her own life as a result.

We had a game plan in place. She would return to California, reduce her belongings down to a transportable level, and start saving money. She was stuck in the apartment lease until the end of December and after that had a place with a family friend she could stay at temporarily.

After Dave graduated to Level Two, he would give it a couple of weeks and then mention our hopes to have Danielle return to us in January. If the judge said yes then she would fly out one way and she and I would drive out the first week of January, pick up her belongings and return home. There was a possibility that the judge would insist on waiting until Dave was Level Three, a delay of a couple of months, or even Level Four, a delay that would require our waiting until at least mid to late summer.

She had a place to go during that time. A friend of the family had a two-bedroom condo, one room that wasn't currently being used, and she could stay there for little or no rent. This would help her pay off her credit debt and continue to save money.

For the first time in years I felt an easy companionship with her again. Each day she had spoken about moving back and we were getting more and more excited about it. Despite the age difference, she would get to see her little sister grow up and forge a relationship with her. I looked forward to that a lot. We had jumped some big hurdles during her visit, and in the weeks before she had arrived, I realized how proud I was of the woman she had become.

Day 32 – 9/14/2009
Color: Green

"How soon will you and Dave have an answer from the judge?" Danielle asked.

I shook my head, "It's not that easy. First, we need to wait for Dave to be up-leveled to Stage Two. This should hopefully happen the first or second Friday in October. Then we need to wait for at least a week or maybe even two, before we bring it up. Dave's already been told he's asked for too many favors."

The request for him to be able to attend his cousin's wedding and permission to teach his Chi Gung class out of county had both been granted, but it was still early in the program. His good behavior had helped, but the court officials were used to being in control and not letting it go until there was an established track record of reliability from a drug court participant.

Less than five weeks in and his record remained untarnished, except for the missed call-in on Day 3. We just had to continue to keep our noses clean and hope to God the officials would be open to the idea of my grown daughter moving back into the house.

Dave greeted me when I returned home, "Storm clouds are brewing on the horizon." Other participants had reported that trackers had burst into their homes looking for Steinbeck. No one seemed to know where he was, and the trackers had been tight-lipped and serious. Steinbeck's roommate, also in the program, looked grim and rather subdued. No one was saying anything, but it didn't look good.

Little Girl was in jail. She had dropped a dirty UA for alcohol. And Casanova was also in trouble. He and Little Girl had gotten into it at the recycling center and he had also been reported for making inappropriate and unwanted passes at a number of the women in the program.

General anxiety over fellow participants, coupled with a concern about Dave's new NA sponsor who had not been in touch with him over the weekend as promised, gave Dave no small amount of stress. It was a reminder too of how easily others slipped back into old, destructive patterns.

Day 36 – 9/18/2009
Color: Orange and Yellow

P.E.'s birthday was a few weeks away when Dave learned that even a child's birthday party was subject to scrutiny. Another participant had mentioned having a party for his child and the drug court officials had shaken their heads. "You're lucky the trackers didn't see and come by to investigate." One of them commented. She went on to explain that the trackers came by every participant's house at least once a day. If they had seen a group of unfamiliar cars, they would have written all of the license plates down, and if any had been suspicious or had warrants, they would have immediately been arrested, and the host arrested as well for associating with known felons.

"Not just that, but they can come in at any time, take people one by one in another room and search them for drugs or alcohol." She added, "If they had refused, then you would have gone to jail."

Dave relayed this and looked worried. Both of us had visions of deputies crashing the party and scaring the crap out of our family, friends, and their kids.

"Well, you'd best talk to the judge then," I threw up my hands, "because I've already sent out the invitations and we have at least 13 people coming!"

It was a Friday, which meant court and a brief meeting with the judge. Dave took the opportunity to mention that he would like to host a birthday party for his three-year-old in a couple of weeks.

The judge, in a frisky mood, looked over at Officer Wheatfield, "Wheatfield, do you think you can find a clown suit?"

The deputy looked nervous, "A clown suit, your honor?"

The judge smiled, "Yes, Wheatfield. A clown suit. You could use the Breathalyzer to make little balloon animals."

He smiled, "Yes, your honor. I'll get right on that."

She looked at Dave, nodded at him in amusement, and approved his request. The party was on!

Day 38 – 9/20/2012
Color: Blue and Level Four

"Mama, I want a fireman." Sitting next to my daughter at breakfast I nearly choked on the mouthful of oatmeal.

"You want a what?"

"I want a fireman, Mama."

Try as I could, I could not figure out what my daughter was asking for. Finally, I joked, "Well honey, in 15 years or more you can have a fireman. It's perfectly understandable, and really, it's the uniform." She continued to insist through much of the day, getting more and more frustrated that I didn't understand her.

Looking back on it now, I am convinced that she was trying to say that she wanted to be a firefighter when she grew up. When she had a larger vocabulary, perhaps six months later, she began to say that she wanted to be a firefighter, doctor and mama.

It was a Sunday, and Dave's schedule was full of mowing, car maintenance, and homework for drug court. He started it off early by mowing the back lawn and then turned his attention toward some of the activities assigned that week.

"I have to find resources in the community for Anger Management, babysitting and childcare, and money resources for the poor. One public, one private from each category." He headed for the computer and began printing out stacks of information, my Relapse Prevention class." I filled the printer with more paper. It looked like we were going to need it.

Day 41 – 9/23/2009
Color: Yellow and Blue

A grief letter to marijuana? Dave's "Dear MJ" essay was fabulous. I was blown away by my husband's detail and care with the letter. Not because Dave is lacking, because he isn't; he's incredibly intelligent. But his intelligence has always had a handicap, one he struggled desperately with as a child. Dave is dyslexic and operated at a below-grade reading level for most of his school years.

Imagine his third-grade teacher's face when the IQ tests showed he had the intellect of a genius after she had labeled him as retarded.

Despite his vindication, he has struggled with words, and as a result, never enjoyed reading books as much as he enjoys listening to them. And writing? I could barely get him to exchange emails with me. He hated writing! Yet here it was - eight pages of a grief letter to MJ, a.k.a. Mary Jane, a.k.a. marijuana

I read the letter and thought about how far we had all come from Day 1...

Dear MJ,

I think it's time that we talked. You have been in my life for 24 years, actually longer. I don't remember how long ago I first saw you; it might have even been when I was in preschool. You were hanging out with the parents of my classmates, going to their parties and hanging out in my neighbor's yards. You and I, as you well know, started our relationship when I was 15.

I was on summer vacation in Nebraska. I snuck out one night with Allison to go skinny dipping in the public pool. The cops showed up and Alli and I escaped to one of her friend's houses. We waited in the basement for some time to pass and someone introduced me to you. I was surprised to find you so far away from San Francisco, but there you were. I was scared of you and pretended to indulge. I pulled a Clinton, even though it wasn't called that back then. You know, "Smoked, but did not inhale". We made it back to Alli's grandmother's house after midnight, no one the wiser. Was that really 1984?

It was a while before I saw you again, maybe late 1985. Oh, I knew you were around. There was the time that my buddy Hiro took a hit of acid before class. He asked me to try to keep him out of trouble, you know babysit him. It was during Announcements, when the entire school, all 60 of us from 6th grade to 12th, was in the main room. Terry, the principal, would go over the events of the day, birthdays, schedule changes, etc.

I looked across the room and saw that you were sitting in Hiro's lap. He was rubbing his fingers over you, right out in the open! I felt my heart jump into my throat. I had promised that I would keep him from doing something stupid. If he was caught, he could get kicked out of school, maybe even go to jail.

I walked over and, as smoothly as I could, I moved you into his calculus book and closed the cover. His first reaction was to jump up and get mad. "What the fuck are you doing?" shouted Hiro. "I'm saving your ass!" I whispered through gritted teeth. "Now sit down and shut the fuck up."

Hiro, as you probably well remember, was a 6-foot-tall, 220 pounds, Japanese-American behemoth. He had 18-inch biceps and was into death metal. Venom, Angel Witch, and Mercyful Fate were always playing on his Walkman. He wore a black leather jacket covered with band patches and steel spikes. His straight black hair fell to his waist. All in all, he looked like an evil giant next to my 5 foot 6, 120 pounds.

The hardest music I listened to was Depeche Mode. I should have known then that you were trouble, but I looked up to Hiro. He was one of the cool kids. He went to rock shows and was invited to all of the parties. I, on the other hand, went home right after school every day and played Dungeons and Dragons on the weekends with my two friends. We drank cherry cola and ate Funyuns.

Hiro looked around the room and realized that everyone in the room was silent and staring at us. He sat down and let me take the text book with you in it. I hid you in my lunch bag as soon as Announcements were over.

After school, I rushed out of the building and gave you back to Hiro. I was so scared all day long that I would get caught with you. After it was over, I said that I didn't want to see you ever again. Even as I was saying it, I could feel that some dark part of me didn't agree. Instead, it felt exhilarated. I had broken school rules and had gotten away with it. On the bus ride home, that part of me kept going over it again and again, "That was exciting!" it said. "Anyway, lots of people smoke pot. It's not like it hurts anyone."

By the next day, most of the "cool kids" knew that I had gone out of my way to save Hiro. They were all impressed and my status level jumped. Suddenly I was being talked to by the popular kids, even confided in. It was great.

About a year later, I was watching **Macross** with two of my friends. You remember **Macross**, right? It's that Japanese cartoon about the giant, city-sized space ship? Never mind. I was with Pat and Ted, that's the important part.

Jabir, John, and Bob came into the room and asked Pat if he wanted to go down to the bleachers and smoke a joint with them. We saw Ted's dad drive up. Ted grabbed his bag and movie from the VCR and headed to the door. "See you all tomorrow," he said over his shoulder.

Pat gathered his coat and bag and stopped, looking at me. "Guys," he said, "Let's bring Dave with us." He turned to them with a sly smile on his face. "What do you think?"

"Great," said Jabir, "You up for it?" He asked.

"Sure," I said.

I was nervous. I knew them, but had never been asked to do anything with them out of school. We walked out of school, across the park, and over the fence to the bleachers. They were owned by the Catholic school down the block, and as such, we were trespassing. John took you out of a Sucrets box and showed you off. I had never seen you so close before. You were alien. You sparkled in the afternoon sunlight. I could smell you from two feet away, exotic and spicy. He ground you up with his fingers and rolled you in a Zig-Zag. Did you know then? Did you know that I would love you forever?

"Um, guys," I said. "I've never done this before. I… I don't know what to do."

They looked dumbfounded. "Never?" asked Jabir.

"Well, no." I said.

They all exchanged glances and started to laugh. "Don't worry about it," John said.

"Just watch us, you'll figure it out." John lit you with a Bic lighter. He rolled you around to make sure that you were lit on all sides evenly. He handed it to Jabir and let out a slow stream of smoke from his mouth and nose. He made a sound that was a mix of ecstasy and relaxation. It was sort of like the sound people make when they lower themselves into a hot tub. Jabir took you and inhaled in five or six short inhalations. He puffed out his cheeks and held in the smoke, his eyes closed.

Pat, now holding you in his fingers, his hand in an "OK" shape, thumb and pointer finger making an "O" with the rest of the fingers pointing up, looked at me and said, "Don't drop it and don't take too much." He had known you for some time and was aware of how unforgiving you are of those who think they are more than your match. He took a small hit and passed you to me. I watched him exhale slowly and smile, his eyelids slowly drawing closed. I took you gently, not wanting to look as scared as I was feeling.

I brought you to my lips and slowly drew you in. I panicked and blew you out as soon as I felt you in my throat. I waited. Nothing happened. I looked around at my friends, my eyebrows pulled together. "It…

didn't work." I said. "Did I do something wrong?"

Patrick smiled as he answered me, "Don't blow it out so fast. Take another hit." I did, this time drawing more of you in and holding my breath for several seconds.

I'm not sure that I can explain you to people who have never experienced you. It was like I was smiling all over my body. I felt light and trouble-free. I didn't care that the girl I liked hardly knew that I existed. I didn't care that my dad had started coming home later and later from the bar. I didn't care about the fact that I didn't know what I wanted to do when I was out of high school. I was content. It was love at first smoke.

I didn't want any more of you, so I watched as they finished the joint. We all climbed the fence and walked to the bus stop. On the bus, I started wondering if I was sleeping. The bus seemed so strange. The dimensions seemed off somehow, as if distorted. The people all seemed odd as well.

They were all in their heads, thinking about the work day that had just ended, about what they were going to have for dinner, or what they were going to watch on TV. I felt as if I had been given the ability to see into them. I felt compassion for the people who were sitting alone, joy for the couples holding hands, and pride for the girl reading a textbook. I rode the bus, looking at all the buildings and wondering who had built them, who had lived in the houses, how their lives had moved on, leaving the houses as reminders. I remember wondering if houses had memories, if they remembered all the birthday parties, and fights, all the move-ins and move-outs. I wondered if they missed people when they left.

   I got off the bus, still in this strange introspective mood. I walked the two and a half blocks to my house, looking at the sidewalk and the power poles, the front gardens and the trees. I had been granted insight into time itself. I could feel the flow of lives and years. It was as if I had spent my life with my head in a cardboard box and I had just figured out how to take the box off of my head. I had never felt so alive in all of my days.

   I got home and sat in front of my window with the late afternoon sun on my face and read some of a paperback that I had bought the weekend before at a garage sale down the block. It was "Sailor of the Seas of Fate" by Michael Moorcock. I understood how the sickly albino, Elric of Melnebone, last emperor of a dying elder race felt as he picked up the magical sword, Stormbringer, for the first time. His sickness faded away and power that he had only dreamed of was now in his grasp.

The part of the story that was lost on me until only a few weeks ago is that he paid a great price for the power. The sword drank souls, you see, in order to give him the power that he was feeling. It had a mind of its own and its own agendas. The sword would allow him to do extraordinary things, but it also destroyed everything that he held dear. It would start out as a boon and end up taking everything from him; his family, his love, and eventually, his life. He couldn't see that the blade was, in fact, a demon.

Like Elric, I only saw the first part and thought of you. I wasn't able to see the rest of the way down the road to see how our relationship would turn, how it must surely end. All I felt was the love.

As the weeks went by and we spent more time together, I started to spend more time with the cool kids. We would go to John's house every Friday, his room packed with people. At 5 p.m. the local classic rock station would always play the reggae song "Smoke Two Joints" by the Toys. We would smoke you and plan our party filled weekends. They would get beer and I would smoke you more. I didn't like beer at all; thought it was really bad as a matter of fact. Sometimes they would do coke. I really hated coke. It made everyone in the room into instant assholes as soon as it showed up.

    I tried mushrooms and found that I didn't feel as much in control when I used it, so it became a "special event" drug. Reserved for camping and events where I was safe and had a babysitter. None of the people I knew were doing anything harder than coke at the time and for that I'm grateful.

    There was a girl named Christine Sandfort in school with me. It had been rumored that she liked me and I must admit that I had sensed her attraction to me for a while. I liked her well enough, but she wasn't part of my new crew. She was bookish and quiet, not at all like the girls I was seeing with my friends. The new girls were more likely to ask if you wanted to do a naked body shot from between their breasts (though they never offer such delights to me) than to ask if I had read anything from Asimov or Heinlein. So, I let it slide. I never pursued her and chose to chase you, MJ, and the girls that I couldn't get.

    I remember how I partied with you all night long before I had to take the SAT tests. I did so poorly that my parents and family wondered if there had been a mistake somewhere. My sister had gotten 1590 on her SATs and I had only scored 1100. They wanted me to take it again, but I refused. I got a job making and selling T-shirts to tourists at Pier 39 in Fisherman's Warf. I was a good salesman and was up for a promotion, but it would have meant more hours away from you. They even hinted that I might need to take drug tests. I quit at once and started going to City College of San Francisco. Again, I resented school for getting in the way of our time together, so I left that as well.

    I had been taking saber fighting classes and had made some friends who also knew you rather well. One girl, Amber, knew someone who had a lot of access to you. His name was Mark and he was one of the smartest people I had ever met. Despite the fact that he never left his house and looked a bit like Jabba the Hut, he was a genuine Master Chess Player. He had global ranking and had games playing with people all over the world. He had several boards set up and would snail mail moves back and forth to people in the East Coast, South America, Europe, and the Soviet Union. We would talk about nanotechnology, spy novels, and most of all, you, MJ.

He had a friend, Will, who was starting up a company that manufactured amplifiers for the TV and radio industries. I went to work for Will and quickly found myself employed as a production manager. One day, Will came down to production (it was in the dugout basement of his house) and asked me if I smoked you that day. "No, Boss," I said, "I haven't been smoking."

He nodded and looked pensive. "Did you smoke yesterday? You did. Didn't you?"

"Yes," I replied. He nodded again. "Do you know what time you left work last night?" I shook my head, honestly not knowing. "It was after 7 p.m. Today, you took an hour and a half for lunch. And now you have shut down production and it looks as if you are going home, even though it is only 3:30."

I didn't know what to say. See, I had been planning to go to see Mark and get a big bag of you, MJ.

"Tell you what," Will said, "You can keep a supply of pot here, in the lab, and you can smoke it whenever you want. Just keep it hidden and if we get inspected, you need to bury it in the yard until they are gone."

I was overjoyed. He understood our relationship. He valued what you had to offer me. Later, while still at that company, I met and started dating Rebecca. Do you remember her? We were married in 1995. We left Will's company under hard feelings over a pay dispute and moved about an hour north of San Francisco.

I started working at a microbrewery and with my new schedule our marriage quickly eroded. They wanted me to work from 3:00 p.m. to midnight. She was working as the receptionist at a telephone company. We hardly saw each other during the week and on my time off I was with you and our new friend, beer. She didn't understand the bond that we had and was jealous of my affection for you both. She had tried to join us. She even suggested that I stop seeing Mark and start to grow you myself.

Truth be told, beer and I weren't that new of friends. My brother won me over with his homebrewed craft beer in 1990 and I had been enjoying it ever since. It was at the brewery, though, that I started take it to the next level. I would drink five or six 22-oz bottles each and every day. In ten months, I had gained fifty pounds.

I was fired from the brewery for insubordination. Those bastards were jealous of my brilliant ideas. I knew that I needed to make money, so I got a grant from the state and began studying to be a PC Tech. During that time, Rebecca started staying out later and later with "friends" from work. I was just about to graduate when she told me that she had been sleeping with a co-worker for the last several months. I begged her to stay, but she said that our relationship had died several months before, that even though she still loved me, that she wasn't "in love" with me anymore.

She left me and I sat alone in my cottage for two weeks, not eating and only taking water when I had to, maybe once every other day. I thought about slitting my wrists and writing "Goodbye Cruel World" on the walls in my blood, but I know that it was just the melodramatic, attention-

seeking side of my nature wanting to be heard. I wasn't answering my phone and two of my friends got worried about me. They showed up and found me in yellowing underwear on my couch. They made me take a shower and put on clean clothes. They took me camping, insisting that I eat food, drink beer, and smoke hellacious amounts of you. They wanted me to howl at the moon until I got it out of my system.

Then I went back to my house, cleaned up the mess, and listened to my phone messages. I had gotten a job and it was starting the next day. Back to the grindstone.

I wasn't able to talk to any females. I couldn't look them in the eyes. I was afraid of them and I hated them all. I would introduce myself as "Hi. I'm Dave. My wife left me." It never failed to drive them away. I dated one girl for a short time. When she admitted that she had spent the weekend having unprotected sex with two guys that she had met in the bar for meth, I wasn't angry, shocked, or even sad for her. I realized that I didn't give a damn if they had slit her throat and left her for dead. I went home, back to you, MJ, and didn't speak to her again except for once on

MySpace. I never looked at my MySpace account again after that contact.

In 2000, I was working for a satellite communications company. We specialized in helping companies to lease and use satellite bandwidth to transfer large amounts of data from one office to another. My manager asked me what I was doing for Thanksgiving week.

"Seeing my family in San Francisco, I guess. Why?"

"Because I think I want to go to Europe. Amsterdam, specifically. I want to be a judge at the Cannabis Cup, the biggest pot festival in the world."

Hearing that, all I could say, with stars sparkling in my eyes, was, "Wow." I bought a ticket.

We were in Europe for two weeks. We spent one week in Amsterdam, smoking more of you than I had ever tried to smoke before and then one week in Belgium. I have never been closer to you than then. We had the time of our lives. I did better in Belgium and after two weeks, I was on a plane again heading back to California.

Months passed and my company was downsized from thirty employees down to five. I was suddenly out of work during the biggest down-turn that our economy had seen since the 30's. It was the dot com crash and there were no jobs to be had and no money left. I would spend my days at my brother's house, cleaning and making dinner. I washed clothes, made beds, did dishes, and shopped from lists that he and his roommate would prepare. They kept me in beer and made sure you were always around in exchange for my efforts.

One of the friends who came to get me from my house after my marriage collapsed offered me a temp job at the architectural company he worked for as an archivist. It was down in San Jose. I remembered that I knew a girl who had moved to San Jose, Christine Sandfort, the girl from high school. I was lonely and I have to admit, looking for a booty call. I tried to find her in the phone book and had no luck. Then I looked online and found her through Classmates.com.

Fast forward a few years. Christine is now my wife and we have a little girl. I had been growing you in our basement off and on for a few years. I chose to upgrade the lights I used for growing you. It cost over $1,000, and even though I didn't have a job it seemed like a good idea. I was followed home from the store and the police were saying that if I didn't let them into my house without a warrant that I would lose my car (so what), my house (big deal), and all my stuff (I have too much shit anyway). Then they drop the real bomb. "We will take your daughter and you will never see her again as long as you live."

All I could say to that was, "Come on in."

Now, MJ, you are the only thing that has stayed with me through the good times and the bad. We have known each other for most of my life and we have been closer than lovers for 24 years. With all that history, you might find it hard to believe that it is over between us. Please believe me when I say this. I didn't want to see you go at first, but there is nothing you can offer me to rival my love for my daughter.

They came in with their video cameras and their guns. They took you out of here and I thought that all traces of you were gone. I had started to forget about you until I went to California to see my family. But there you were, hanging out with all of my old friends. They didn't understand why I would walk out of the room when they pulled you out of their pockets. They even followed me, asking me what my problem was. It was hard to see you again, but even though I longed for you, the repercussions of us being with each other again vastly outweighed any temporary benefit I might get from you. You were being pushy, demanding.

I came back determined to have you out of my life for good. There were a lot of people who didn't believe that I could stay away from you. They said, "No one can walk away from that long of a relationship just on willpower alone." But I cleaned away all signs of you, even had my house inspected by an agent of the Missouri court system. I was sure that you were gone.

Then I found you hiding in my tool chest. Beautiful, purple hair, and smelling so sexy you made my heart flutter. That was a low blow. It felt as if my house had been invaded. You just sat there, as if nothing had happened between us. As if you had not endangered everything that I hold dear. You were willing to walk back in here and put my life at risk again. Fine, maybe you didn't walk in, I'll admit I let you stay and had forgotten.

Well, my dear, this is it.

As I dumped you down my kitchen sink, into the garbage disposal, I felt the pull of *our past, I will never forget how good those times were, but I also can't forget how dark things have been as well. Like in that paperback book from so many years ago, you gave me a feeling of escape from my pain. If only you hadn't charged such a heavy price, you awful bitch.*

As I poured bleach down my kitchen sink to wash away any last trace of you, I felt like the bad guy in an Edgar Allen Poe story or even an episode of CSI. I felt like I was disposing of your body to give me a clean start and to lay my claim to a new beginning.

Goodbye, MJ.

Day 44 – 9/26/2009
Color: Green and Blue

Dave left early so that he could pick up another participant he had promised rides to. Allen's color was blue, so they both needed to submit UAs at the sheriff's office in Harrisonville. Dave looked pained that evening as he described not being able to pee for nearly 45 minutes and after THREE tries. The officers razzed him significantly over this.

It was Saturday and at noon the drug court participants were taken to the Cedar Cove Animal Sanctuary as a treat. The sanctuary was home to lions, tigers, and other wild creatures of the feline persuasion. Two coatis, members of the raccoon family, had escaped and were nosing about on top of several of the cages.

Dave had brought the camera and snapped plenty of pictures for us to see.

Day 45 – 9/27/2009
Color: Orange and Blue

"I'm miserable; got any ideas on what I should take?" Dave stared at me morosely. I had been moving like a whirlwind through the house, dusting and vacuuming and snapping orders. He hadn't complained, just helped move the chairs and put the dishes away as I zoomed from room to room. Sundays typically end up as cleaning days in our house. Both Dave and P.E. were obviously suffering from either a mild cold or allergies. P.E. couldn't stop coughing and Dave couldn't stop sniffling.

"I have no idea what you can take." He couldn't take any kind of drug that induced sleep, caused wakefulness, or anything that could be used in the making of meth, so that ruled out most over-the-counter medications. And since we didn't have medical insurance, he was up a creek, without the proverbial paddle.

He sighed, "I'm going to go to CVS and ask one of the pharmacists."

"That sounds like a good idea. Hey, pick up some name-brand cough medicine for P.E. since she refuses to take the generic." I called after him as he left.

She had pronounced both of the generic pediatric cough syrups "yucky" and refused to take them. So much for cutting corners and saving a few dollars. Dave just nodded and headed out. Twenty minutes later he returned with meds for both of them.

"I was honest with the pharmacist and explained that I was in drug court and limited on what I could take." He said as he patiently tried to convince P.E. to swallow a dose of name-brand cough medicine. She was hiding in a corner and shaking her head.

"She asked me what drugs I was in for and when I told her pot she looked shocked and asked me, 'The courts put you in with meth users?!'" He shook his head, "That sure blew her mind."

"What did she give you?"

"Zyrtec."

"You'd better call Sherrie and …"

"Already did. She said Zyrtec was on the acceptable meds list and thanked me for calling."

I smiled at him and turned back to my research on recidivism of drug court participants.

Later that evening he groaned, "Awww ..."

"What?"

"The GABF (Great American Beer Fest) is going on in Denver this weekend." He sounded depressed, but chuckled when he read the next email, "Oh look, someone wants to send me a million dollars."

"Cool. Are they from Nigeria or Mugabe?"

"Can't tell, but the guy says his name is Dr. Monarch, that sounds like an evil villain for sure."

"Or an evil butterfly."

Day 50 – 10/2/2009
Color: Orange

Friday…court day. Today Dave would be up-leveled into Phase Two and his obligations to drive to Harrisonville reduced to 2 ½ days per week instead of five. He had scheduled an interview for Saturday with a friend who owned a home health care company who had promised to give him as much work as he could handle. I kissed Dave goodbye, convinced that he would return happy, with the next day free to help me prepare for P.E.'s birthday party. I dropped her off at daycare, drove to work, and spent the day getting my friend and boss ready to go out of town for the next week. She treated me to lunch and I returned home excited.

I had shared the news of Dave's transition to Phase Two with her, and practically everyone, convinced it was a sure thing. Dave had spoken about it with his counselors there at the drug treatment facility and they had all assured him he was a green light to go to Phase Two a week early. Up-leveling can only occur on the first Friday of each month, so it would be this day or we would have to wait until November 6th.

Dave didn't look happy as he walked in the door. "Sit down; I have to talk to you."

Oh no ... "Please tell me you were up-leveled to Phase Two."

"I wasn't." My heart sank. I sat down on the couch slowly.

P.E. was pulling on my hand, desperately wanting my undivided attention, and undoubtedly sensing something was wrong. Dave went on to say that really, he didn't have any other information. The judge had ignored him, the drug court team had refused to say anything to him, and he was in the dark as to why he had not been up-leveled.

Day 56 – 10/8/2009
Color: No Action

Sonia had heard from Dave that I taught parenting classes and wanted to meet with me. After two weeks of clashing schedules and phone tag we had set a meeting up for 5:30 that evening. It would give Dave enough time to return from Harrisonville, pick up P.E. and for us to eat together. I drove down to Cass County Psychological straight after dinner. I was nervous; I wondered what Sonia would be like in person. Especially after just hearing the stories of Dave's experiences, I didn't hold any of the counselors or drug court team in very high regard.

She was small, maybe five foot two and probably not more than 110 pounds. Sonia had red hair and a genuine smile and I felt a little better. It was a strange situation to be in, but I had wanted to meet her for two reasons – the first was to promote my parenting classes and newly formed company Families Indeed, the second was to support Dave by showing her, and consequently the rest of the team, that I was an intelligent, well-spoken, thoughtful, caring wife and mother. This would further cement their vision of us in the weeks and months that would follow. It would help distinguish us as different, worthy of trust and respect, and hopefully ease Dave's way through the program.

We talked at length about parenting principles and techniques and discussed the format of the classes and how they each built on the other. Sonia looked excited and very interested in the program. It seemed that my enthusiasm for the subject was contagious.

Day 71 – 10/23/2009
Color: Yellow

The judge was in a particularly fine mood that Friday. She spoke at length of how everyone was progressing in the program and how proud she was of everyone's efforts. After nearly 30 minutes of discussing everyone, in particular Little Girl's efforts to stay in the program despite her many slip-ups, she called Dave's name first. Each participant speaks with the judge personally there in court in front of the other participants.

She looked over her notes, "Well, Mr. Shuck, I see nothing but outstanding comments about your conduct and participation lately. Also, I see that you are volunteering your time with other participants to help with GED prep study. We are all impressed by your level of involvement in this program and have decided to reward you for your efforts. If you continue to provide this help you will no longer be required to perform your monthly community service. Also, if you continue to put in the number of hours that you are currently putting in we will use that as a credit toward the number of hours you must be at Cass County Psychological each week."

Dave thanked her and she paused and smiled at him. "And Mr. Shuck, in light of recent developments in legislation in certain states, I hope that, after the holidays we can engage in a lively debate about certain possible changes in the legal status of marijuana."

Just a few days before had come the news that California and New York were both considering legislation that would make the consumption of medical marijuana legal in their respective states. There had also been an announcement from the Obama administration that drug raids would be limited to only those who were producing marijuana in excess of the allowed amounts in those areas of the nation where it had been decriminalized or legalized.

Dave and I, along with many others, viewed it as a large step toward decriminalization and the eventual legalization throughout the country, one state at a time. I only hoped that Dave could hold his own with the judge and not find himself in a precarious situation that might prevent him from being up-leveled in the future. I likened it to dancing with a cobra. The judge had such power and control that it frightened both of us. How would Dave handle this?

In just a few short months he had gone from actively resenting the program to focusing on learning and growing from the experience. Others had seen it, commented on it, and recognized his efforts – but we remained all too aware of the power and control the drug court officials had over our lives. We had learned to take nothing for granted and to trust only in a limited fashion what they told us. It was this lesson, reinforced each day, which would determine every step we made for the remainder of the program.

Day 78 – 10/30/2009

Color: Orange

We were both awake early on Friday morning. Court started at 8 a.m. and Dave typically left at around 7:15 to pick up Allen and drive down to Harrisonville so they would arrive with plenty of time to spare. I checked email and then headed into the kitchen to make coffee and share some time with him before he left. I was looking forward to my free day; I had a lot of writing and classes to finish updating.

Weighing heavily on both of our minds was next Friday, Day 85, the first Friday of the month and the hopes Dave would finally be up-leveled to Phase Two. Allen, a meth addict and alcoholic who had been enrolled in the program three weeks after Dave, was also scheduled to be up-leveled.

We wouldn't know for a week more if Dave would be up-leveled. It seemed likely, overwhelmingly so, but after being denied up-leveling at the beginning of October neither of us was making any kind of plans until it actually happened.

Dave began to discuss his work in the GED prep program. Approximately one-quarter of the drug court participants had not finished high school and the drug court was encouraging (or in some cases, mandating) that they obtain their GED before graduating the drug court program. Dave had volunteered to help with the math and social studies portion and already had several students. Lacking even an outdated copy of the GED prep workbook, he had begun with helping one girl study the Emancipation Proclamation by reading through it line by line. By breaking it down, one sentence at a time, he turned a relatively complicated document into one that made sense, "I am the president of the United States ... I have certain powers in time of war ... here is what I'm going to do ..."

We talked at length about the attitudes and limited ways of thinking that both sides, drug court participants and drug court officers, fall into. In particular the 1971 Stanford Prison Experiment[1] was weighing on our minds. This study had been alarming in that it showed how quickly we can degrade into abuse, coercion, and lose all empathy and even dispense with our personal moral code when put into a prison environment. Although Dave and the rest of the participants were not incarcerated, except when they broke one of the rules in the program, the mentality seemed to carry over to some degree. Drug court officials viewed participants as sneaky, untrustworthy, and incapable of trust.

In some cases, it seemed to be a 'damned if you do, damned if you don't' scenario. Dave received many conflicting messages, "Be honest, tell us everything," which he did only to hear, "We hear the same thing every time. You have a set number of stories you never vary from." I laughed when I heard his response to that particular comment.

"You're right, I've *never* told you about the time I had drunken sex with a dead bear." When the counselor's eyes widened in shock he continued, "That's because it never happened. You asked for the truth, I've told you the truth and the stories never change because, unless you want me to lie, there aren't any more stories to tell!"

Intellectually we understood that most of the participants would lie about their skin color if they thought they could get away with it, much less anything else, but it was frustrating to be included within that group and be treated daily with such distrust. Instead of letting it get to him, Dave continued to reiterate the same thoughts, emotions, self-history, and to be as authentic and patient as possible. We both realized the burden was on us to prove ourselves trustworthy. It was up to us to show everyone that we were different, that we were willing to learn what the court wanted us to learn and follow the rules and succeed in the program. Whether they believed we were telling the truth at all times or not, we had to be our authentic selves and fully embrace the situation we were in.

Already his work in the GED prep class had been recognized in court by Judge Baker who commented that his continued participation would mean he did not have to perform the minimum requirement of four hours of community service per month. A boon, since the community service had typically occurred on his days off, which had meant even less time at home with us.

Day 82 – 11/3/2009
Color: Orange and Green

Apparently, the drug court officers were not informed that Dave had been moved to a Level Two in the treatment process. When Dave's color came up on Tuesday, he called his probation officer Sherrie to make arrangements to submit a UA here in Belton, rather than drive down to the Harrisonville Sheriff's office. She was surprised and asked him what he was doing out of treatment. She seemed a bit put out when he explained and said she would be making calls, which of course, alarmed both of us. But by the time he showed up at her office all was fine, she had just been caught by surprise and was annoyed at being left out of the loop.

Sherrie admitted, "We all realized that we wanted to keep you at Level and Phase One because your presence has made such a difference with the other participants. The staff at treatment have really enjoyed being able to take everyone on trips recently since they don't act like ..."

"Like crazed monkeys?" Dave finished.

"Exactly." Sherrie smiled. "But that's not fair to you. You have earned this and you will be up-phased to Level Two on Friday and very possibly we will up-phase you to Level Three on schedule if not a little early if things go well."

Day 85 – 11/6/2009
Color: Orange

Dave was finally up-phased to Level Two. The judge seemed happy and even The Director (one of the drug court officers who had dressed Dave down in the past) had nice things to say. Finally, we felt a sense of relief. We had moved into the next stage, one step closer to the ultimate goal of graduation!

Marijuana – Its History and More

> "There's no way to rule innocent men. When there aren't enough criminals, one makes them. One declares so many things to be a crime that it becomes impossible to live without breaking the laws."-Ayn Rand in Atlas Shrugged

Marijuana is not a new drug. Man has used it in one form or another since before we progressed past the Stone Age. Having it as an ancient companion doesn't necessarily make it good – modern man endured fleas and lice at the same time and that certainly wasn't a bonus. But cannabis has been used for many things – marijuana for its relaxing effects and ability to promote appetite in those who have little or none and the fibrous hemp for its myriad of practical uses.

There are also many pre-conceptions and erroneous assumptions that our country has in regards to cannabis. This is due in no small part to the propaganda program we have all been exposed to since the early part of the 20th century. That means that there is no one alive today, born in this country, who has not been told at one time or another that this "terrible drug" will:

- Turn you into an addict
- Provide a gateway to other addictive substances
- Drive you insane
- Cause you to be violent
- Make you into a criminal

Thanks to the War on Drugs, the last one is absolutely true. As for the rest? Well, why don't we start with a little bit of history first?

A Companion through History and Pre-History

Marijuana has been used since before recorded time and cultivated for just as long. According to ProCon[2], which features a historical timeline, marijuana has been in use, in one form or another, as far back as 5,000 years of recorded human history.

Here are the Chinese symbols for Ma, or hemp: 大麻. The symbol beneath and to the right of the straight lines represent hemp fibers dangling from a rack. The horizontal and vertical lines represent the home in which they were drying.

As far back as Chinese Emperor Fu His, (ca. 2900 BC) "there have been references to Ma, noting that Cannabis was a very popular medicine that possessed both yin and yang."

Cannabis pollen has been found interred with Egyptian mummies, is purported to have been an ingredient in ancient holy anointing oil, and has been used for centuries as a curative for a host of maladies including treatment for glaucoma, earaches, inflammation, and much more.

> "Well, I have zero desire to smoke pot. I have in the past, but I'm past it. But I want legalization because I believe the drug war is one of the major causes of several problems in our society, including violent crime, police misconduct, over-incarceration, forfeiture abuse, self-treatment of mental illness, and many others." – Ben C.

The Constitution of the United States of America is written on paper made from hemp and at least two American presidents cultivated hemp on their plantations.

Cannabis, Hemp, or Marijuana?

So ... wait a minute ... hemp ... cannabis ... marijuana ... is it a drug? Is it a fiber for making rope? What are the differences?

The best term to describe it all is cannabis. Cannabis is a genus of flowering plants that includes Cannabis sativa, Cannabis indica, and Cannabis ruderalis.

Cannabis ruderalis

Cannabis ruderalis is low-growing and produces protein-rich seeds which can be used in culinary and even personal care products. It is very low in THC (tetrahydrocannabinol) the compound that induces the proverbial high that marijuana users seek, so it is not grown for industrial, recreational or medicinal use.

Cannabis indica

Cannabis sativa and Cannabis indica differ from each other in the following ways:
- Cannabis sativa has higher levels of CBD (cannabidiol) and is also where the hemp strain comes from (low concentrations of THC and high concentrations of CBD).
- Cannabis indica is known for its sedative qualities
- Cannabis sativa provides a more "cerebral" high that pairs well with physical activity, social gatherings and creative projects.

Most varieties of cannabis are hybrids of the sativa and indica strains.

Cannabis sativa

Here is a table[3] that illustrates some of the modern uses for the cannabis plant:

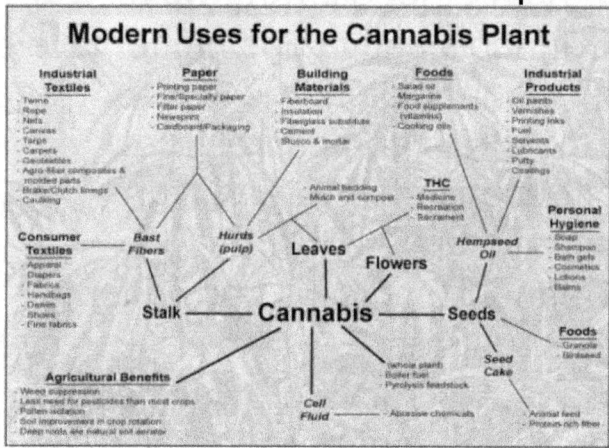

If you have difficulty reading it, you can find a copy of the table by doing a simple Google search on "Modern Uses for the Cannabis Plant"

Cannabis indica and Cannabis sativa are both higher in THC, and in addition to producing a high, are also responsible for several therapeutic uses, which include:

- Reduces depression, elevates mood

- Relieves headaches and migraines
- Energizes and stimulates
- Increases focus and creativity
- Reduces nausea
- Stimulates appetite

Of the approximately 2,000 cannabis plant varieties known, approximately 90% of them contain only low-grade THC and are most useful for their fiber, seeds, and medicinal oils. In other words, most of these are hemp.

According to the North American Industrial Health Council, "If one tried to ingest enough industrial hemp to get a buzz, it would be the equivalent of taking 2-3 doses of a high-fiber laxative." In other words, you would crap your pants long before you felt an inkling of a high.

Despite cannabis and human history being intertwined for thousands of years, both in the industrial sense and the recreational sense, it is currently illegal to grow any form of cannabis in the United States. Apparently, the U.S. Drug Enforcement Agency, the State Department, and the Federal Bureau of Narcotics are incapable of telling the strains apart (despite the obvious differences in appearance and THC levels).

Addictive … Or Not?

One of the many arguments going back and forth is whether or not marijuana is addictive. Keep in mind that there are physical addictions and psychological addictions. For example, if you are a regular morning coffee drinker, and you miss your daily dose of caffeine, what usually happens? The mother of all headaches, irritability, even sluggishness. You become used to that daily dose of stimulant. Take it away, and your body reacts. That's a physical addiction right there.

Some drugs may be psychologically addictive as well, but answers on psychological addiction vary by country (hint, the U.S. will tell you that marijuana is psychologically addictive while other countries will not) and by the individual. For example, does the individual exhibit signs of compulsive behavior? This compulsive behavior might lend itself to a stronger psychological attachment to the feeling (emotional or physical) an individual experiences while using a particular drug.

In a purely anecdotal sense, I have seen two long-term marijuana smokers use the drug over a period of ten years and 20 years, respectively. One stopped and started, as money or circumstances interfered. The other refused to cease smoking under any circumstances ever. Both engaged in what I would consider compulsive behavior – but were they *addicts*? I don't think so.

Compulsive behavior can become addictive behavior, but in the case of marijuana, we must tread carefully. Drug education programs are lumping the two behaviors together and saying they are the same. This is inaccurate. Worse, we are sending our children the wrong message and, as a result, garnering the exact opposite in results.

California Superior Court Judge James P. Gray, author of *Why Our Drug Laws Have Failed and What We Can Do About It* writes, "Children are often told that marijuana is highly addictive and that long-term marijuana users often develop a chemical dependence that makes withdrawal difficult or impossible without professional help. These children find out soon enough that this message is untrue, which serves to discredit the messengers. When we spread untruths about marijuana, our children learn not to believe us even when we tell them the truth about such drugs as methamphetamines and cocaine."[4]

Again anecdotally speaking, I have seen a long-term marijuana user withdraw from it and stop cold turkey after years of smoking daily. He was slightly grumpy for a few days and that was it.

So ... Why Is It Illegal?

I'll give you the short answer – money, racism, fear-mongering and control. Here is a longer answer ...

> "The Nixon campaign in 1968, and the Nixon White House after that, had two enemies: the antiwar left and black people. You understand what I'm saying?"
>
> "We knew we couldn't make it illegal to be either against the war or black, but by getting the public to associate the hippies with marijuana and blacks with heroin, and then criminalizing both heavily, we could disrupt those communities.
>
> We could arrest their leaders, raid their homes, break up their meetings, and vilify them night after night on the evening news. Did we know we were lying about the drugs? Of course we did."
> – John Ehrlichman, former aide to President Nixon

There is an excellent timeline at Drug War Rant[5] that details just how it came about – but two central figures appear to be the prime movers and shakers of the push to ban not just marijuana, but all forms of cannabis.

Those men were Harry J. Anslinger and William Randolph Hearst.

In 1930, a new division in the Treasury Department was established-the Federal Bureau of Narcotics-and Harry J. Anslinger was named Director. Anslinger was an extremely ambitious man, and he recognized the Bureau of Narcotics as an amazing career opportunity-a new government agency with the opportunity to define both the problem and the solution. He immediately realized that opiates and cocaine wouldn't be enough to help build his agency, so he latched on to marijuana and started to work on making it illegal at the federal level.

Here are some of his quotes on marijuana...

"There are 100,000 total marijuana smokers in the US, and most are Negroes, Hispanics, Filipinos, and entertainers. Their Satanic music, jazz, and swing, result from marijuana use. This marijuana causes white women to seek sexual relations with Negroes, entertainers, and any others."

"... the primary reason to outlaw marijuana is its effect on the degenerate races."

"Marijuana is an addictive drug which produces in its users insanity, criminality, and death."

"Reefer makes darkies think they're as good as white men."

"Marihuana leads to pacifism and communist brainwashing."

"You smoke a joint and you're likely to kill your brother."

"Marijuana is the most violence-causing drug in the history of mankind."

Anyone notice the rampant contradictions? Apparently, you can go insane, have relations with another race, be a criminal, be a *pacifist*, and kill your mother – wow, anything is possible when smoking the reefer! And if one racist hater wasn't enough, enter William Randolph Hearst onto the stage. Drug War Rant puts it quite succinctly:

"Hearst had lots of reasons to help. First, he hated Mexicans. Second, he had invested heavily in the timber industry to support his newspaper chain and didn't want to see the development of hemp paper in competition. Third, he had lost 800,000 acres of timberland to Pancho Villa, so he hated Mexicans. Fourth, telling lurid lies about Mexicans (and the devil marijuana weed causing violence) sold newspapers, making him rich."

Hearst was making money on both ends. He was the father of yellow journalism, and his newspapers published lurid, sensationalist lies about the effects of marijuana in order to sell more newspapers. These newspapers were printed on paper made from the timber industry that he controlled. Some of the stories were so markedly absurd, one wonders how readers of his newspapers could possibly believe such tales. Here are just a few of the quotes from his newspapers:

"Marihuana makes fiends of boys in thirty days — Hashish goads users to bloodlust."

"By the tons it is coming into this country — the deadly, dreadful poison that racks and tears not only the body, but the very heart and soul of every human being who once becomes a slave to it in any of its cruel and devastating forms ... Marihuana is a short cut to the insane asylum. Smoke marihuana cigarettes for a month and what was once your brain will be nothing but a storehouse of horrid specters. Hasheesh makes a murderer who kills for the love of killing out of the mildest mannered man who ever laughed at the idea that any habit could ever get him ..."

"Users of marijuana become STIMULATED as they inhale the drug and are LIKELY TO DO ANYTHING. Most crimes of violence in this section, especially in country districts are laid to users of that drug."

The account of how quickly the legislation was passed is absolutely mind-boggling. This, despite the fact that a doctor, Dr. William C. Woodward, Legislative Council of the American Medical Association, testified during the hearings that all claims of AMA endorsement of making marijuana illegal were manufactured and erroneous. His arguments were ignored and the Marijuana Tax Act of 1937 passed.

Only in America

The prohibition against growing hemp in the United States is nonsensical at best, and tragic at worst. Hemp grows quicker, without pesticides or fertilizers, than cotton. It makes more ecological sense to raise hemp for paper than harvesting trees for paper.

France and Spain have never stopped growing hemp. And in the early '90s England and Canada officially recognized the differences between hemp and marijuana and legalized the growing of hemp in their countries.

On June 11th, 2012 the CEO of Dr. Bronner's Magic Soaps, David Bronner, locked himself in a cage outside the White House with a pile of hemp plants and equipment, intending to make enough hemp oil to spread on a piece of French bread[6]. Dr.

Bronner's imports over $100,000 in hemp oil from Canada each year to make its popular soaps. Bronner's protest had two points, a) the restriction of growing hemp in the United States is foolish, and b) American farmers are losing hundreds and thousands of dollars in potential income from the production of hemp. He never got the chance to complete the oil-extraction process and enjoy his bread before the police sawed through the bars and arrested him. "Bronner was charged with possession of *marijuana* and blocking passage." You see, in America we are apparently too stupid to understand the difference between hemp and marijuana. Good job, boys in blue.

As odd as it might seem, hemp oil, hemp seeds, and other processed hemp products (clothing, paper, rope and more) are perfectly legal imports. From a sustainability viewpoint, this seems pointless and possibly disastrous. Why are we paying to import what we could easily produce ourselves?

Hemp is easily grown, requires little or no pesticides even on a large-scale production model, and is an inexpensive, better alternative to a multitude of monoculture crops currently grown in the United States (corn, soybeans, and cotton to name a few).

The War on Drugs in America

In the United States the War on Drugs is devastating our population on several different levels. It has led to the erosion of our civil rights, created skyrocketing incarceration rates, increased corruption in our state and local governments (most particularly in law enforcement), and demonized drug users as criminals of the basest nature. I want to cover these briefly and suggest additional reading for those interested in learning more.

Erosion of Civil Rights

First and foremost in my mind is the erosion of our civil rights. From undercover sting operations, stakeouts at local hydroponics or farm supply stores, wiretapping, and the extensive use of snitches, the War on Drugs takes an increasingly invasive approach to reducing our civil liberties each and every day.

Judge Gray writes, "Faced with an ever-worsening drug problem, and the public alarm that accompanies it, the courts, albeit without design, have grudgingly but consistently allowed our Bill of Rights protections to be eroded in exchange for what is hoped to be progress in the war against drugs. Judges are human and when faced with a choice between weakening the protections of the law 'just a little bit' in order to make progress against this overwhelming problem, they unconsciously have been 'doing their part.'" [7]

From approving questionable warrants to be issued, to allowing wiretapping or accepting the hearsay of informants – judges do their part to erode civil rights – and we are losing the freedoms at an exponential rate we have held so dear for over 200 years.

Drug court itself is an exercise in exposing its participants to widespread civil rights violations. Later you will read about a man who was incarcerated for nearly two weeks due to an erroneous un-calibrated Breathalyzer. He lost his job, and suffered repeated humiliations from drug court staff and Judge Baker over a two-week period until the lab results came back negative, just as he said that they would.

The fact that, according to the documents of the court, I also gave up my rights to unreasonable search and seizure by occupying the house with a drug court participant, or that David was required to give up a perfectly legal drug (alcohol) in order to participate in the program, were all deliberately designed to eat away at our civil liberties.

So, what civil liberties were infringed upon? I'll list them out.

First Amendment – freedom of speech – while a participant in drug court, Dave was required to "tell the truth at all times" – but what that really meant was, "Say what we want to hear or we will punish you if you disagree." That is not freedom of speech.

Second Amendment – the right to keep and bear arms – while in the program we were not allowed to have firearms present in our house. Despite the fact that we have the right under the second amendment, while in a drug recovery program, not parole, we were banned from retaining any weapons for our own defense.

Fourth Amendment – protection from unreasonable search and seizure – while a participant of the drug court program we were informed that if we denied a visiting tracker the right to search through our home, cars or person – it was an automatic stay in jail for Dave. Even if a tracker came by when I was alone in the house, if I refused them entry, they would consider it a violation and punish Dave with jail time.

Fifth Amendment – due process, double jeopardy, self-incrimination, and eminent domain. In order to be allowed into the program, Dave was required to first plead guilty to all of the charges against him. It was a great unknown – we had no idea what the drug court program would entail, but if it was unreasonable in any way (which it was) we would be subject to punishment within drug court or his guilty plea would be enforced with possibly the maximum sentence allowable under law.

At one point, one of the counselors in the program who was kinder to us than most said to me, "I really question the constitutionality of drug court in general. Really, if all of what happens came to light in a court of law, in front of a Supreme court, surely they would rule that drug court is completely and totally unconstitutional and in violation of [Dave's] and your civil rights." Not surprisingly, the counselor didn't last long before he sought out other employment. Before he left, he told Dave that he simply could not agree with some of the tactics used in the drug court program.

Skyrocketing Incarceration Rates

> "As a retired CIA analyst who spent 31 years following European issues, I am struck by the fact that the US (population 313 million) has more people behind bars for drug crimes (about 500,000) than all of Western Europe plus Canada (population 450 million) have incarcerated for any reason (486,000).

> *And our overall incarceration rate is 716 per 100,000--the highest in the world--while the rates in those other Western countries range from 58 in Finland to 147 in Spain. (Data from the World Prison Population List, 10th edition, 2013) So either Americans are the most criminal people on the planet, or we are incarcerating too many of them."* – Richard K.

We have become a nation recognized worldwide as having the highest documented incarceration rate in the world. According to *Breaking the Taboo*[8], a documentary on the failure of the drug war, our nation's total population comprises approximately 5% of the total world population, but in the United States alone, the total number of incarcerated individuals represents 25% of the total number of incarcerated worldwide.

We aren't the land of the free anymore. *We are the land of the imprisoned*.

More than any other country in the world, including China, we were at the top. As of 2008 a study produced by King's College London reported that in the "land of the free" there were 756 adults incarcerated per 100,000 citizens[9].

In 1994, it was reported that the War on Drugs resulted in the incarceration of one million Americans each year.[10] Of the related drug arrests, about 225,000 are for possession of cannabis, the fourth most common cause of arrest in the United States.[11] In 2008, 1.5 million Americans were arrested for drug offenses. Of these, half a million were imprisoned.

Marijuana constitutes almost half of all drug arrests, and between 1990-2002, marijuana accounted for 82% of the increase in the number of drug arrests. In 2004, approximately 12.7% of state prisoners and 12.4% of Federal prisoners were serving time for a marijuana-related offense.

According to *Breaking The Taboo*[12], the number of incarcerated offenders has risen from 330,000 in 1970, to 2.3 million in 2000.

<u>Increasing Corruption</u>

> "You say it's a waste of money, but that's not the case for everyone. It's down to cheap, square-headed greed for all those who benefit, if they are even aware of this dimension of the problem...the politicians are smart enough to be aware, and there's the real problem." – R.I.

Make no mistake, the War on Drugs means the opportunity for law enforcement, lawyers, and the industrial prison complex to make big-time money. It is a siren call, corrupting officials and encouraging the acceptability of what can only be described as legal theft.

First and foremost, there is asset forfeiture. I described this earlier, but I really want to reinforce the lesson that we learned. Essentially, if you are *accused* of a crime then your assets can be seized and sold, even without any *conviction* in a court of law. Countless travelers have fallen victim to this. Traveling with cash, anything from a few hundred dollars to thousands is often considered an 'indicator of criminal behavior' and cash and vehicles are confiscated without any due process.

In our case, all of the lights, the ionizer that helped cut down the smell of the plants, and anything of any value that was directly related to marijuana production was confiscated and sold – long before our day in court. What is interesting though is the fact that while 13 plants were confiscated, only ten were reported as seized. We had ten almost dead harvested plants and we had three healthy ready-to-be-cloned plants. I'll leave it to you to figure out what happened to those remaining three.

When you give any individual or group of people the power to confiscate an individual's assets – cold hard cash, expensive equipment, et cetera – you open the door for graft, corruption, and greed. That's a fact. We can point to the individuals on the police force, or the judge who accepts bribes, or the county commissioner, or a host of others as being the "bad apples" – or we can recognize that the system of asset forfeiture is endemically flawed.

As a country, we have also put into place a 'prison industry' that places more value on incarceration than rehabilitation-in all areas of criminal behavior.

In the past 30 years we have nearly quintupled the number of prisoners in the United States. There are entire towns built around massive prisons-earning tax revenues that power their infrastructures, their schools and public parks and roads. Towns that would crumble to the ground and blow away if the prisons were gone- for the prisons are the main employers, and the source of income for countless shops and stores that provide services for the employees of the prisons. With those kinds of motivations, the graph above turns into an advertisement, unlimited earning potential for dying townships. And on the heels of that comes corruption-why not incarcerate American citizens for the slightest offenses? The more that are in prison, the more money that flows from the prisons into the pockets of millions of support staff-suddenly, incarcerating others is *lucrative*.

Cheap labor is a big incentive as well. Angela Davis, author of *Masked Racism: Reflections on the Prison Industrial Complex* explains:[13] "As prisons proliferate in U.S. society, private capital has become enmeshed in the punishment industry. And precisely because of their profit potential, prisons are becoming increasingly important to the U.S. economy."

In other words – incarcerate a large amount of the population and then use them as cheap labor. Employ them in call centers placing reservations for American Airlines or AVIS, for example, and pay them far less than minimum wage. Why outsource to another country when you get them for cheaper than a Third World sweatshop's going rate?

How cheap are we talking about? According to Rania Khalek, author of *21st Century Slaves: How Corporations Exploit Prison Labor*,[14] "Over the last 30 years, at least 37 states have enacted laws permitting the use of convict labor by private enterprise, with an average pay of $0.93 to $4.73 per day. Federal prisoners receive more generous wages that range from $0.23 to $1.25 per hour."

This line of thinking, this deeply disturbing way of doing business, draws a dark, black line between the general populace and the incarcerated, creating a distinct sub-class of people. This class of people who already find the odds stacked overwhelmingly against them. These same people who may inevitably return to prison instead of being rehabilitated or even avoiding incarceration in the first place.

Demonization of Drug Users

> *"I spent 5 years in Federal Prison for a marijuana offense. While I was there, I watched armed bank robbers come and go in as little as 20 months. After 3 years 'behind the wall,' I pointed this out to the parole board. Their response: "You must understand, yours was a very serious offense." How do you respond to that mentality?"* – Hugh Y.

Our country is approaching drug use from a crime and punishment angle and ignoring its human aspect. Judge James P. Gray wrote[15]:

"It remains a critical part of our zero-tolerance policy that people who use illegal drugs cannot be considered in human terms. They must be treated as demons and we must contrast 'drug cultures,' on the one hand, with 'decent' people, on the other. We are also led to assume that these 'junkies' are always dangerous. It was no slip of the tongue when Daryl Gates, former chief of police of Los Angeles, said that 'casual drug users should just be taken out and shot,' or when 'Judge Judy' is reported to have said while on a speaking tour in Australia that her answer to the free needle program, which was trying to reduce the spread of disease associated with intravenous drug use, was to 'give them dirty needles and hope they die.' The unmistakable message to the public is that drug users are to be feared and scorned."

Is there no middle ground? Can we not recognize the differences in drugs, their effects, and possible addictive (or non-addictive) qualities? Must we categorize everything in black and white? And while some might say that this applies only to the "hard drugs" – from the behavior of law enforcement, drug court officials, and many, many others – the label of drug user carries a huge black "X" of shame on anyone it is bestowed upon.

So, there you have it. I've given you a short history of marijuana, the War on Drugs, and the incarceration and *abuse* of literally millions of our citizens. If you aren't angry, then I would suggest that you may need to re-examine your priorities. This is happening to your neighbors, family members, friends, and the citizens in your community. The system is deeply broken and it is steadily growing worse with each day that passes.

Phase Two

Day 89 – 11/10/2009
Color: Green

"Sherrie told me today that I would be required to get a full-time job no matter what I was doing with the Chi Gung classes," Dave reported, looking frustrated. He had just returned from the local probation office where he had gone to submit for the UA.

"She says it doesn't matter how much I make with the classes. If I'm not working a full 40 hours a week teaching then it won't be okay with the judge."

I thought for a moment and remembered his comments about Allen, who had also been up-phased at the same time as Dave had. He had relayed Allen's fears about having so much time on his hands instead of being in classes all day.

Allen was also looking for work but, unlike Dave, he had no real work experience. He had spent most of the past few years selling drugs. With little or no experience in a 'real' job, he was unsure what he was qualified to do. Figure in the bleak offerings of jobs in the current economy and Allen definitely had cause to worry. He was also still struggling with overcoming his addiction to meth.

The reasons that drug court insisted on full-time work was probably two-fold – they were intent on filling the participant's time with activities (whether in treatment, through community service, or actual income-generating work) in order to keep them away from the temptation of drugs, and that was probably the number one motive. The second motive was to encourage the participants toward an active role in the community. Becoming a productive member of society is usually identified by a 'regular job' and 'regular hours,' and whether those hours were filled at night in a warehouse or flipping burgers during the day didn't really matter; it was all considered good, honest work.

Both of these motives were reasonable and expected. We understood the drug court's reasoning, even if they hadn't explained it completely, and were now faced with the decision to conform or make our case for different treatment.

As Dave and I discussed it, we recognized that the most likely motives behind Sherrie's words were the concern of relapse and that Dave be a productive member of society. We made the decision to make a case for Dave's teaching Chi Gung and building his business. I pointed out that it wasn't just teaching a class that was considered work; there were probably 3-4 hours of work in marketing and promotion each day toward the goal of expanding classes and hours throughout the local community.

Day 108 – 11/29/2009
Color: Orange and Blue

Damn, damn, and triple damn. Dave forgot to call in on Sunday and earned a 48-hour stay in jail. He woke me up at 10:30 p.m. the evening before in a complete panic.

Two weeks passed after Dave's 48-hour "shock time" with little to report. None of the drug court participants were misbehaving, and life had begun to have some semblance of normalcy as we settled into Phase Two.

Day 122 – 12/13/2009
Color: No Action

P.E. went with my mom and we went out shopping to Half Price Books and Dave said he was starving. We settled on the Macaroni Grill and, when seated in the back of the restaurant, I asked Dave if it would be safe if I ordered a margarita. He said no, unless I wanted to sit at another table. I then felt awful for asking and he felt bad for having to say "no." It made me realize that no matter how close to this I am, I can never fully understand. What I was asking for was asinine. If someone had caught us, even though it was my drink, not his, he would be put in jail for SIX days and possibly be down-leveled back to five days a week and unable to work or watch P.E. How could I put us in that position? How could I even think that it would be okay to bend the rules?

Day 128 – 12/19/2009
Color: No Action

Swimmer found the BBC website and called Dave. The BBC website (Belton Brewing Company) had been crafted by me, in the days before the bust, when we were dreaming of pursuing Dave's goal of opening a brewery. It had not been touched in ages, well over 18 months, but this would not matter to the drug team. While you are in drug court, all drugs, legal or illegal, are completely off the shelf. To have a website promoting even the *idea* of us producing alcoholic beverages was unacceptable.

Before Dave entered the program, Swimmer, also charged with marijuana production, was considered the "golden boy" of the program. From what we could tell this mainly consisted of telling the judges and drug court officers anything they wanted to hear and keeping his head down. You would not hear any arguments for the legalization of marijuana from Swimmer's lips. He had his eyes on the prize – get done with drug court as soon as humanly possible by telling them what they wanted to hear and by keeping his mouth shut the rest of the time-except when faced with the opportunity to make himself look even better.

We had just given him the perfect opportunity.

Day 130 – 12/21/2009
Color: Green

Swimmer reported the BBC website to Fingers, one of the counselors in drug court. Dave was told that he needed to take down the information immediately, especially the pictures. This was done minutes after Dave came home and told me of the problem. He was later told he was lucky he wasn't sanctioned. Sanctioning would have included jail time.

He expressed his frustration in his individual counseling session with Dr. Maid. Unfortunately, Dr. Maid was Dave's outgoing therapist. He was leaving the drug court program the next day. Dr. Maid spoke to Dave frankly and cautioned him to watch what he said. "Some of the counselors here are zealots; be careful what you say and do."

Day 140 – New Year's Eve
Color: Green and Phase Four

The discussion in group had turned heated the evening before. The group was talking about expectations and asked if anyone had any expectations that they simply would not let go of. Dave mentioned me wanting to live in an old house and he said he was going to do his best to see that I got one.

"No, no, no," one group member said, "Wanting things that we cannot achieve is what made us turn to drugs in the first place, you must set your sights on *realistic* goals."

Dave brought up the example of Thomas Edison, "He tried and failed numerous times to create the telephone, the lightbulb; should we have told him to give up and be reasonable?"

"That's different."

"How is it different?"

"Thomas Edison was a professional; he was brilliant."

Immediately my mind raced with names of brilliant individuals who had been failures or had labels attached to them. Abraham Lincoln, who ran for office multiple times, and finally succeeded, eventually becoming one of our country's most revered presidents. I thought of Albert Einstein who, despite speech difficulties, went on to become a brilliant scientist. Should either one of those men have given up, accepted 'reality' and embraced mediocrity?

    On one hand I understood the argument they were making ... be realistic, don't lose yourself to 'pie in the sky' dreams because that kind of thinking leads to disappointment, depression, and especially in most of the drug court participants, drug abuse. But Dave and I strongly objected to the dual message of, "get a job, any job, work 40 hours a week, come home and don't dream. After all," they seemed to say, "It is all you are really capable of anyway."

    Having just finished re-reading one of my favorite books by James Hogan, *Voyage from Yesteryear,* I was incensed by this restrictive, closed-minded idea. Dave said to them, "To suggest to any of us that we are incapable of better things, that we must set our sights low and expect less from our lives ... At best, you are being oppressive. And at worst, you are being criminal."

They didn't like hearing that. And I figure that is too bad. To hell with them, for after all, they are the exemplification of failure at worst and mediocrity at best. What could they possibly know about reaching for your dreams?

Day 151 – 1/11/2010 – Dave's Birthday
Color: No Action

One of the counselors in the drug court program is named Fingers. Well, that's not her real name, obviously, but we called her that due to the rather chilling story we heard about her own past. Early on in the program Dave had come home and told me about this so-called counselor. I say 'so-called' because Dave was absolutely sure she had zero degrees and only some kind of certificate program (less than an Associate's) to her name and was part of a team of counselors who met one-on-one and in group with the drug court participants.

Fingers had shared her history of addiction one day in group. She had apparently reached a desperate stage in her addiction to meth, which had led to owe her drug dealer a large sum of money. She was told that her debt could be paid if she did a favor for him. Apparently, there was another woman who owed quite a bit more money, and he wanted something in return.

Fingers lured the woman out of the bar, grabbed a sharp knife or hatchet and *cut off the woman's fingers to get to her rings.*

When Dave told me this story, I could not believe it. That kind of thing doesn't happen, does it? Months later, Fingers recanted her story, claiming she only beat the woman up and made her give up her rings. I don't know which story to believe. Honestly, that isn't really the point. The point was that this woman, a former addict who was violent toward another to some degree, without any formal training, was now acting as counselor in the drug court program. How was that helpful in any way?

Day 153 – 1/13/2010
Color: Yellow and Blue

We were now being actively threatened with the possibility of Dave not being up-leveled to Phase Three. Sherrie asked for proof that Dave was working for me helping out with the cleanings. I called her and asked her what exactly she needed and asked if a letter would suffice. She said yes, and added that Dave would need to get a *third* job (on top of working for me and teaching Chi Gung) to bring his weekly work hours up to 40 or he wouldn't be allowed to up-level.

Day 157 – 1/17/2010
Color: Orange and Blue

A tracker came by last night. It was Deputy Good Old Boy, and Dave greeted him at the door and said, "It's been so long since I saw any of you, I went out and bought a keg and a new bong. You wanna see?"

Deputy Good Old Boy blinked and asked, "Did you really?"

"No, do you want to check?"

"No."

"Really?"

Deputy Good Old Boy just grinned and said, "Hey I've got people I've still got to see that I *will* need to check out. Do you really want me to come in?"

Dave said, "Sure, I do."

"And that's exactly why I don't need to."

He then asked why Dave wasn't Phase Three yet.

Day 159 – 1/19/2010
Color: Orange and Yellow

Dave began chairing two Narcotics Anonymous meetings a week. This shows additional responsibility, commitment, and dedication to his 'recovery.'

Day 164 – 1/24/2010
Color: Blue

Deputy Good Ole Boy came by late, around 11 p.m. We are normally in bed, but all of us had had a nap that afternoon, and P.E. had slept for over three hours. He came in, shot the breeze for a while and asked Dave about his Chi Gung classes. He told Dave that, when he comes up for a vote to Phase Three, Dave has definitely got his vote.

Day 165 – 1/25/2010
Color: Orange

We began work on the hall bathroom remodel and completed most of the demolition. In the weeks to come we would end up installing a tile floor, painting the walls, replacing the fixtures (including the lights), upgrading the plumbing, and converting an antique dresser with a raised sink. The toilet was now in the bathtub and the linoleum has been pulled up and removed. We had also discovered a rotted board which needed replacing.

As part of the lead-up to qualifying for Phase Three, Dave was required to show an increase in hours worked so that drug court could see that he was gainfully employed. At least one of the drug court officers, his probation officer Sherrie, seemed unwilling to recognize that owning a business means more than just teaching a class for a few hours a week. It also means billing, marketing, and plenty of meetings and promotions. It meant constantly attracting new people since not everyone is going to take a class and become a permanent student.

Dave had to prove his investment in Kansas City Chi Gung by logging his hours, along with the hours he spent working for my cleaning business.

He had set up several meetings for the week ... Tuesday afternoon at Penn Valley Community College, Wednesday afternoon with the Cradle of Love, and was working on meeting with a coordinator from Johnson County Parks & Recreation. The last one could be a dead end, although she was very interested in Dave at the time. One of the affiliates with JCP&R had signed Dave up to teach Tai Chi, then had run a background report and discovered that he had charges pending against him and told him that it is their policy to not employ anyone with a record or even pending charges. They then assigned the class to another instructor.

We hoped that a face-to-face meeting and full disclosure up front would help with this problem, but I wasn't holding out hope. No matter what, Dave had other meetings and would have other victories, but this was a challenge no matter where he went if they did any kind of a background check.

Day 166 – 1/26/2010
Color: Green and Blue

My fear that Dave would not be approved to up-phase grew significantly with Dave's report on a second disastrous counseling meeting with the new counselor, Labels. He had made the mistake of speaking his mind and letting her know that it would take a while to adjust to her as his new counselor. He mentioned trust issues and this was immediately latched onto as a main focus of the therapy sessions.

When he presented his homework, she marked him down as a zero because he had not accounted for his week in some kind of graph format. She then asked him about his homework from the week before, which had been to list his strengths and weaknesses. She had been unhappy with his list of weaknesses, feeling apparently that it was too short of a list. He hadn't known what to do to make it better and said so, so she marked him down as incomplete for that homework as well.

Later, as he talked about a home bathroom remodel project and all of the details of that, somehow it turned into her labeling him a perfectionist.

I saw quite clearly one of the glaring problems that Dave continued to run into-our shared wish for understanding and acceptance. We want others to know *who* we are. But in situations such as this, understanding and empathy only work to a certain extent. And in some cases, Dave's openness was being used against him. It was not a good idea to speak his mind, and he regretted it deeply each time he did.

Day 168 – 1/28/2010
Color: Yellow and Green

Dave brought his business plan, class schedule, and projected income estimates to Sherrie in order to have it ready for court tomorrow. Sherrie, who had seemed dead-set against accepting Dave as a business owner, insisted he somehow come up with 40 hours a week of work and appeared at least somewhat impressed by the paperwork. We continued to hold out hope that Dave would be allowed to up-level to Level Three. This would probably mean an additional day off, either Friday or Monday. We were aiming for Fridays off. Having Fridays free would allow Dave to offer a noon class at a local hospital and also an afternoon slot for the local libraries.

Day 169 – 1/29/2010
Color: Yellow and Blue

Friday was Court Day and it was an unmitigated disaster. Allen was reamed for losing his job. He lost his job because of his past driving record. He was driving classic cars from one warehouse to another at a local auction house. When the DMV check came back, they let him go.

Dave was up next and the issue of incomplete homework came up. When Dave was asked about it he tried to explain. He got about five words in before one of the prosecutors on the drug court team began screaming at him. When he tried to respond, he was screamed at for interrupting, the very thing the man had done to him in the first place.

Attention fell on his business plan and he was asked if his students all knew he was a drug addict. He responded, "I'm not teaching a drug addiction class, so no, they are not made aware of the situation."

The court responded that this was a "big problem" and then they asked if Tai Chi/Chi Gung promotes a healthy, drug-free lifestyle and he lied and said "yes." This, of course, brought up the question of how he had done it for the past 20 years while smoking pot and drinking. When he admitted that was true, they said again that they had a "big problem" with that.

The judge ripped up his business plan in front of the entire court, telling him that his priority was drug court, not his family, not his business, not his own personal life. She then sent him back to his seat.

After court he approached Lieutenant Large, the head of the sheriff's team to speak to him about one of the deputies at the jail who had not been following protocol when doing the drug/UAs on drug court participants. He would not flick on the Breathalyzer until a participant was out of breath and would then yell at them to 'keep breathing' while asking them if they wanted to go to jail. He also did not test the UA in front of the participant, a strict violation of policy. He could create a 'false dirty' if he wanted to, because he orders the DC participant to the pit while he tests the urine. Dave had been having a significant amount of trouble with this guy because he does not drink large amounts of soda pop like the rest of the group and his pee is light yellow or nearly clear. The guy always accuses him of watering down his urine in order to pass the drug test.

As he approached Lieutenant Large, the judge ordered him back in front of her. "You must think at times that this court is out to get you, don't you, Mr. Shuck?"

"Yes ma'am, it does appear so at times," Dave pantomimed her shredding his business plan.

"I did that for effect, Mr. Shuck. I have a copy of your business plan in my files. I have a question for you. If you lie to me, you may not make it to group today." She glared at him, the threat of jail and sanctions an obvious possibility. "And I will know if you lie. We haven't talked lately and there has been some recent legislation towards legalizing marijuana. Tell me, Mr. Shuck, what your stand is on this legislation?"

Dave looked her in the eye and said, "Your honor, I believe that the war on drugs in regard to marijuana is unjust and immoral. I support legalization of marijuana. That said," he paused, "I believe that just as an alcoholic should stay out of the bar, so I should avoid using marijuana."

She shook her head, "That's what I thought you would say. Go to treatment, Mr. Shuck, I'll see you next week."

Dave then spoke to Lieutenant Large, who nodded and said he had heard this from other sources as well and that he would address the situation that day. Dave then headed for treatment.

Immediately upon entering, Sonia ordered him into her office and said frostily, "You are to begin family counseling with Labels immediately, starting next week." When Dave asked how long it would last, she said, "It will last as long as it lasts, perhaps until you complete the program. Now I believe you have a class to go to."

Dave walked into class and it was being headed by Director, the ex-addict turned counselor who had delayed Dave's up-leveling for five weeks to "see how he handled the pressure." As the class started, Director turned to Dave and smiled, "So Dave, I'm sure you have something to 'process' regarding your week."

"No. Not right now. I'm going to process what happened in court today by myself and speak to my wife about it tonight. I think I will be better able to discuss it on Monday."

Director sneered, "Afraid you are going to dig yourself a deeper hole?"

"No," Dave replied in kind, "I'm afraid I'd take a shovel to your head."

For some reason this hostile response and inference of a threat actually made the guy laugh. "That's more like it!" He left Dave alone after that.

Later, Fingers called Dave aside. "I heard what happened and for what it's worth, if I had been there, I would have stood up for you. I understand why you have trust issues; after all, it was proven today you have good reason not to trust us."

Was Fingers an ally? Not likely. After months of dealing with their machinations, I believed that this was all an elaborate game. It was designed to break a drug court participant, to show them how helpless they were.

The lessons they learned were many, and none of them particularly positive. They did not build people up or give them hope for a better future. They knocked them down onto the ground and then kicked them hard in the ribs and head while their victim lay there stunned and in shock.

This wasn't the first time a drug court officer had said, "Oh, if I had been there, I would have spoken up for you." They were all full of shit and they were all liars. That was the lesson for the day.

I called my dad and updated him. He was pissed, especially over the issues of "get a job, but you have to tell them you are an addict" crap. He came up with a plan to get Dave employment for whatever hours were needed to fill it up full.

He advised me that he knew people and that they would be willing to say Dave worked for them and that yes, they knew he was an addict. We decided to simply give up on the Chi Gung biz until drug court was done. We would still try and build the business, but we would simply stop talking about it.

Day 170 – 1/30/2010
Color: Orange and Green

We were both depressed and frustrated and resentful. Mainly we kept coming back to the question of how we could turn the situation around and somehow impress the court with our positive attitudes. All the while we quietly dreamed of leaving this place when drug court was done and we could move to Central California and raise pounds of marijuana on a self-sufficient eco-farm.

I couldn't help dreaming of how we could raise specialty crops for local restaurants of heirloom fruits and vegetables, and fund it all with the marijuana operation. To hell with drug court and their control freak ways – we were determined to survive and eventually escape their clutches.

Day 172 – 2/1/2012
Color: Yellow and Blue

Dave went to treatment yesterday and a part-time counselor named Jessa was heading a group therapy class and she saw him and asked, "Dave, I heard that you had a difficult time in court on Friday; would you mind sharing with the group what happened?"

Dave had had enough time to process through what had happened and he gave an account of what had occurred. Others in the group offered their take on the judge shredding his business plan, suggesting that what she had been trying to say was that if he didn't take drug court seriously, he was in essence shredding his own dreams of owning a successful business.

Jessa took this all in and after class barged into Sonia's office demanding verification of what happened to Dave in court on Friday.

Sonia admitted that yes, the judge had shredded his business plan in front of him and yes, then the rest of the team had taken turns tearing him down further. Jessa was quite upset by the treatment she saw Dave and others receiving. A few weeks later she tendered her resignation.

Day 175 – 2/4/2010
Color: Orange and Phase Four

Sherrie was furious at Dave when he called and notified her that he would be going out of county to purchase an electric chainsaw in Buckner. As she railed on him, he realized that the reasons for last Friday's court drama were more than just zeroes on homework. The drug court team had been angry at him for neglecting to provide goals on *all* facets of his life (NA, drug court, treatment, and his business plans).

Either he had misunderstood their requests or they had not specified them effectively. No matter, the problem was in his court. He immediately drew up detailed goals for all of the areas and dropped the paperwork, including copies of our tax returns, to Sherrie.

He had included a note at the bottom of the goals expressing apologies if there had been any miscommunication with the court regarding the paperwork, he had turned in the week before and explained that he had simply been providing them with business goals only.

Sherrie seemed pleased with the paperwork and inferred that not everyone was against him starting his Chi Gung/Tai Chi business and that up-leveling to Level Three was not completely out of the question for court the next day.

I remained cautiously optimistic and asked Dave to call me the next day as soon as court was out. If he was promoted to Level Three, he could be eligible for up-leveling to Level Four as soon as the first Friday in July. And if that went well, he could be looking at a possible graduation date of early to mid-December.

Day 176 – 2/5/2010
Color: Green and Blue

No up-leveling for the month. Which meant that we were looking at January 2011 as the earliest possible graduation date. After all we had been through, we weren't holding our breath.

Day 181 – 2/10/2010
Color: Yellow

I met with Dave's counselor Labels for the first time. I found her to be a very dangerous person.

At the onset of the meeting for the mandatory family counseling she sat down across from us and said, "I'm sure you are aware that if I feel you are not a positive influence for Dave that I can tell the judge you and Dave should live apart during the course of his involvement in drug court. How does that make you feel?"

I paused for a moment, shocked that this woman had just threatened me. As if that would have any positive effect, or encourage me to open up to her in any way. Where had this person gotten a counseling degree? What idiot had let her graduate?

I took a quick breath and plastered a confused look on my face, "I guess you could do that." I shrugged, "But I can't imagine why, so I don't even know how to answer that."

I managed to smile, somewhat, enough to turn my face into a complacent mask. It would not do to try to outsmart this awful creature, or to show my intelligence over much.

That meeting's beginning dictated the remainder of our family counseling relationship. I did not trust her. Nor did I believe she had any counseling skills whatsoever.

She was, and remains, in the best and worst place she could possibly be. It is best for her, because she has actual employment, a marvel in itself. And worst, because she is busy pushing her clients (I prefer to call them victims) into nasty labeled holes all while believing she is actually doing them some good.

I would spend the remainder of our counseling sessions ensuring that a) we always brought P.E. to add to the distraction/chaos factor, and b) I always tried to have at least 2-3 projects or activities I was currently working on to talk about. These took up valuable time that might otherwise have been spent trying to pigeonhole and label us. There would be absolutely no benefit to these counseling sessions – other than to allow me to further Dave's model behavior and cooperative stance in the program.

Day 195 – 2/24/2010
Color: Orange

We met again with Labels. I filled the hour by talking nonstop about our garden (the legal one). We had also made teaching the *Parsley, Sage, Rosemary and Thyme* class a family affair the night before. It had been a great experience and Dave had been quite excited about being able to participate and add to the discussion.

James took Dave aside after counseling to tell him he had been rooting for him but that there were others who are against him. Their reason? They think he is arrogant and a know-it-all. James took a stand against them and won no friends, but stuck to his guns, saying that displaying arrogance or being intelligent was not a valid reason to hold someone back from being up-phased.

Sometimes intelligence can be a drawback. Here was a prime example of it. People don't like to feel stupid. And people in positions of power *really* don't like to feel stupid.

Day 199 – 2/28/2010
Color: Orange and Yellow

A tracker came by today. Deputy Good Ole Boy told Dave that he was in support of him being up-phased next Friday. He mentioned, as James had a few days ago, that there were several people opposed and several people strongly in support of up-phasing.

The objections being voiced were, according to Deputy Good Ole Boy, not very relevant. He told Dave that he fully expected that Dave would be phased up this coming court date.

Day 200 – 3/1/2010
Color: Green

Allen was pulled aside and told that he would be up-phased to Phase Three on Friday. No one said anything to Dave about up-phasing.

Day 201 – 3/2/2010
Color: Yellow and Green

Day off from treatment, so Dave went to the local Belton office to submit a UA. He mentioned that he had heard Allen was being up-leveled and Sherrie told him he would be as well. Hopefully all will be well on Friday.

Day 202 – 3/3/2010
Color: Yellow and Phase Four

It was time for another family counseling session with Labels. She got straight to the point. "You mentioned a few weeks ago that you knew about the marijuana growing in the basement. Tell me more about that." That discussion took up most of the meeting. Beforehand, Dave had asked me to ask for him about up-leveling. Up-phasing is drug court related, and we were informed that Friday was a pretty sure thing at this point. Up-leveling is treatment related and affects how many days or hours per week Dave must be in Harrisonville.

Labels informed us it would be about two weeks since she had already put in the paperwork for it. This was good news since the up-phase and up-level do not necessarily coincide. When P.E. announced she needed to go to the bathroom Dave took her while I questioned Labels more on what hours we might be looking at.

"I'm asking all of these questions because I need to plan our income and expenses. Daycare is expensive; the sooner we can go to part-time, the better," I explained.

Labels latched onto this immediately, her pen busy making notes on the paper. "Oh, are you having money problems? Are you not paying your bills? What bills are you not able to pay?"

There was no way in hell I was going to tell her we had just declared bankruptcy. The papers had been filed the day before. "We are paying all of our bills and we have money in savings still to cover emergencies, but I have to plan for any emergencies, et cetera. There's no point in running out of money and then worrying about how to get it when we can put a plan in place now that will prevent us from having a stressful situation.

Labels gave a nasty, tight-lipped smile, "Well it's probably best not to plan for anything in regards to drug court."

"I understand the need to wait until things happen, but also keep in mind that my host sites, and Dave's, are currently planning for fall classes. So, whether I like it or not, I do have to plan at least 4-6 months in advance.

That's just the way it is. It's the nature of the business I'm in."

We left it at that and moved on to other things.

Day 203 – 3/4/2010
Color: Green

Third time this week for a UA drop. Dave talked again to Sonia and she verified that he would be phased up. She also mentioned that she had noticed him and one other participant had worked until the very end at the dance without complaint. She told him she had waited to see if he used that, drew attention to it, to point out how hard he had worked. That he did not, that he had done it out of a selfless act of community service, had impressed her greatly.

She told him she appreciated his help the past weekend, especially with regard to his enthusiastic and dedicated efforts without prodding from her or the others. Finally, we received the confirmation that Dave was being up-leveled. One step closer to graduation!

Drug Court - A Brief History

Earlier I discussed the accelerated incarceration rate in the United States. As drug arrests in the drug war quickly filled the prisons-there was a serious overcrowding problem. Beginning in the early 1980s, the number began to quickly increase from 500,000 incarcerated throughout the United States to nearly 2.5 million in 2006.

Something had to change. And for the first time, the suggestion of drug diversion as a possible tactic to reducing drug use was implemented. The first drug court, located in Miami-Dade County in Florida, appeared on the scene in 1989. According to the National Institute of Justice's 2006 report[16], "Drug courts emerged in the late 1980s in response to rapidly increasing felony drug caseloads that strained the Nation's courts and overflowed its jails and prisons. Their goal is to reduce substance abuse and criminal behavior and free the court and correctional systems to handle other cases."

> "Drug Court has been an obstacle to my daughter's addiction rather than a treatment. First, the Court decided that my daughter could not live at home because her brother was in another Drug Court. The Judge said "move or go to jail" but my son's Drug Court said it was fine because they are immediate family members.
>
> My daughter works 40 hours a week and has to spend most of what she makes on an apartment. She also has to pay for gas to go to the classes and drug tests and my husband and I must help with food. She was a heroin addict who quit cold turkey at home.
>
> She got a job and just recently got promoted. But the stress is wearing on her and I fear she will go back to heroine after six months of being clean. My daughter is trying in spite of drug court but it is almost like they want to force her back into addiction." – Michele

In this chapter I will cover how drug courts operate, as well as the benefits and drawbacks of the drug court system.

How It Works

So exactly what is drug court and how does it work? You have read my account so far of it, which was of course written from a participant's point of view. Here is the official intent on drug court, taken from the National Association of Drug Court Professionals Drug Court Standards Committee:[17]

In 1997, the National Association of Drug Court Professionals published *Defining Drug Courts: The Key Components* designed to provide courts with a model which can be adapted to fit the specific needs of the community.

The 10 key components:

1. Drug Courts integrate alcohol and other drug treatment services with justice system case processing.

2. Using a non-adversarial approach, prosecution and defense counsel promote public safety. Participants must waive their due process rights to a speedy trial and sign a pre-emptive confession before being allowed to participate.

3. Eligible participants are identified early and promptly placed in the Drug Court program.

4. Drug Courts provide access to a continuum of alcohol, drug, and other

related treatment and rehabilitation services.

5. Abstinence is monitored by frequent alcohol and other drug testing.

6. A coordinated strategy governs Drug Court responses to participants' compliance.

7. Ongoing judicial interaction with each Drug Court participant is essential.

8. Monitoring and evaluation measure the achievement of program goals and gauge effectiveness.

9. Continuing interdisciplinary education promotes effective Drug Court planning, implementation, and operations.

10. Forging partnerships among Drug Courts, public agencies, and community-based organizations generates local support and enhances Drug Court effectiveness.

The idea is relatively straightforward – create and enforce a drug-free environment for the drug court participant. Make abstinence from any illegal drugs (and often alcohol) mandatory, keep them out of jail as long as they comply with drug court regulations, and encourage a drug-free lifestyle *after* graduation.

Cass County's Roll-Out

In 2005, Cass County Missouri rolled out the beginning of the drug court treatment program currently operating today. Its goal – to help drug addicts recover from their addiction, to break the cycle of drug use, and often the subsequent criminal behavior that accompanies it, and to transform lives.

According to the 2012 article series in *The Democrat Missourian*:[18]

> *"Eight years ago, Cass County's Drug Court program was a dream that looked good on paper, but could it get off the ground?*
>
> *Cass County Circuit Judge Jacqueline Cook saw the potential – an opportunity to change lives. So did then Presiding Circuit Judge Joseph Dandurand, as did Prosecuting Attorney Chris Koster.*
>
> *But money for training and set-up was then, as now, in short supply ... In 2003, Cook applied for and received a U.S. Department of Justice grant to get the ball rolling. Former Circuit Court Clerk Kelly Elliott enthusiastically climbed on the wagon, as did Sheriff Dwight Diehl, the Cass County Probation and Parole Office, and*

various treatment providers throughout the county, Cook said.

In 2004, the newly formed team underwent training in California and spent months planning for what would be a 2005 launch for the program that has, Cook said, changed an incredible number of lives."

Drug courts sounded like a step in the right direction. It assumed that through counseling, behavior modification, drug education, and more, a person who had been accused of possessing or using narcotics could avoid incarceration and possibly learn to live without drugs.

A recent series of articles in *The Democrat Missourian* detailed the series of phases that a participant must go through in the Cass County drug court:[19]

<u>*Phase One: Stabilization*</u>

The most intensive of the phases, Phase One, includes a full clinical screening, job skills and educational assessments. It is also the most restrictive of the phases, mandating that an applicant stay within county except for court appearances or for work-related duties. Employment during this time is nearly impossible – every day except for Wednesday and Sunday drug court participants are required to be in the treatment center in Harrisonville. There is also the mandatory participation in AA (Alcoholics Anonymous) or NA (Narcotics Anonymous) – with a required attendance of at least three meetings per week. Combined with a 10 p.m. curfew, the focus of drug court is on clearing the participant's system of all illegal drugs and alcohol. This phase lasts at least eight weeks and requires at least 30 days of full sobriety before the participant can transition to the next phase of treatment.

<u>Phase Two: Early Treatment</u>

During Phase Two, the participant is required to obtain employment, or in some cases, be a full-time student. There is some reduction in the number of days required for a participant to attend treatment, but the required three meetings a week in AA or NA is still enforced. Curfew is expanded from 10 p.m. to 11 p.m. During this phase, the participant begins to identify relapse warning signs and develops ways to prevent or reduce relapses. By the end of Phase Two, participants will have been in drug court for at least six months.

<u>Phase Three: Active Treatment</u>

It is during this phase that the participant learns to manage his or her emotions and the rationalizations that lead to poor decision-making. Court appearances drop to once per month and 12-step meetings drop to twice per week. In addition, the curfew extends to midnight. This phase lasts a minimum of five months, with the last 120 days "clean."

<u>Phase Four: Maintenance and After Care</u>

There is a continued required participation in a 12-step program, but only once per week during the final phase of Drug Court.

Meanwhile, the curfew remains midnight, and candidates are expected to maintain employment and work on educational requirements. Monthly individual counseling is conducted.

It is during this phase that the participant may have a role as a mentor, learns to enjoy life and realize all that a substance-free life can offer, according to Bruegge.

The average duration of Phase Four is five months, but there is no minimum.

So there you have it. There are four phases of drug court, with an anticipated minimum of 15 months in the program, and a relatively straightforward drug treatment plan. Cass County has an ambitious, involved program for dealing with non-violent drug offenders. No program is without its difficulties, however. No program is better (or worse) than the individuals who design and run it. Which leads us to …

The Drawbacks

In an era where the terms 'Big Brother' and 'nanny-state' are thrown about with increasing frequency, drug court ranks high in its invasiveness of personal privacy and freedom. Drug court attendees agree to allow drug court officers into just about every facet of their lives. In order to avoid incarceration, they allow drug court officials to control what they do each day in the early stages of the program, to mandating what time they must be at home at night. For most, this degree of control by the drug court officers is comparable, if not worse, to revisiting the teenage years of their youth.

There is definitely a feel of angry parental figure to the whole experience.

Like most public schools, it is also a "one size fits all" mentality. A higher functioning individual is bound by the same rules and regulations as someone who is still lost in the grip of a meth addiction. And while I understand the concept, I simply do not agree with the premise. People are not all the same, and they do not function or thrive in a rigid environment in most cases.

There was also a stark difference between how the rules for going out of county were enforced when Dave entered the program versus when he finally left. At the beginning, all he needed to do was let Sherrie know that he would be going out of county and what he was going for (homeschool event, to help my mother with a home repair project, or pick up some item for sale) and it was perfectly acceptable. During Phase Two or Three, Sherrie went on vacation, and the sheer number of calls she normally received from the drug court participants went to Lieutenant Large. He was not pleased to be receiving so many calls. After she returned, the entire system of going out of county was reviewed and a near total lockdown on out of county expeditions ensued. This became a frustration for us, since it meant that many of the outings that we had planned for homeschool with our daughter (especially the science-oriented outings that Dave was responsible for) had to be canceled. Cass County is not large, and participating in family events in Kansas City itself weas made impossible while Dave was in the program. There was no real good reason for this – why restrict someone from visiting a museum or nature center?

    The Cass County Drug Court team was also quite emphatic that they had the right to decide who a participant could live with, and who they could not. As I mentioned in the last section, this was presented to me in a rather disconcerting manner during our initial family counseling session. It was very clearly a threat in my mind, and thus I was determined to do everything I could to make sure we made a good showing. I didn't want Labels to think for one moment that we weren't the perfect couple, perfectly agreeable and working together toward a drug-free environment for all of us. If there ever was any benefit to be had from our mandated family counseling, I certainly wouldn't experience it, I was too busy ensuring that our wall of unity was completely smooth and unbroken. This wasn't hard; our relationship is a solid one, despite a touch of enabling behavior on both sides. In the end though, there was no benefit from the family counseling for me or Dave personally.

    On the first page of the Drug Court Participant handout it states that drug court is not intended to be a punishment, but rehabilitation. Yet, as Dave stated later in his Application for Graduation, "there remains a firmly embedded model of incarceration, retaliation, and retribution. Always the threat of what will happen if we step out of line looms over us."

    When he gave that application to the drug court officers, at least one of them admitted that there had been a debate over whether or not to punish him for speaking his mind. If the goal of drug court is to encourage sobriety and clean living, through enforced sobriety, education, and self-examination – then how can you have it both ways?

Either you want someone who can think for themselves or you want someone who says, "Yes ma'am, no sir," and follows the status quo blindly. It seems to me that the latter is the type more likely to go back to their friends and resume their drug-addicted lives. The former is more likely to have perspective, a larger world-view, and fully understand the negative influence of drug addiction.

Or perhaps, and most likely, the drug court officers didn't like the thought that somehow, some way, their system needed improving.

A National Debate

Since the advent of drug courts in 1989, and tens of thousands of participants later, the national debate on the efficacy of drug courts has grown.

In 2011, the Drug Policy Alliance published Drug Courts Are Not the Answer: Toward a Health-Centered Approach to Drug Use. The article mentioned several key failings of drug courts:

<u>Drug Court Research is Often Unreliable</u>

There have been a large number of studies on drug courts, but the poor quality of that research is now being examined. John Roman, senior researcher at the Urban Institute was quoted, "The central criticism is that they employ convenience samples or compare drug court participants with drug court failures, in effect stacking the deck to ensure that the study finds a positive effect of drug court."

Drug Courts Often "Cherry Pick" Participants

The article went on to note that "some drug courts may opt to knowingly enroll persons who do not need treatment, but for whom drug court participation is seen as the only way to avoid a criminal record for a petty drug law violation. This may not be an insignificant occurrence. As mentioned previously, about one-third of drug court participants do not have a clinically significant substance use disorder."

And by cherry-picking individuals who do not need this program, who are we leaving behind on a "do not stop, do not collect $200," direct trip to prison? While my husband attended drug court there was one, ONE African American in the program. When you consider that African Americans are 3-4 times more likely to be arrested for a drug offense, don't you think there would be a couple more of them in the program?

Rewards and Sanctions Are Often Disastrous and Inappropriate

> "We all live in fear every day...Will today be the day they take my son for 'dilute' urine...some stranger that stares at his penis and tells him repeatedly if it's clear, you are going to jail. What authority have we given to our criminal justice system to punish the most in need? The only ones walking away feeling good from this nightmare are the police." Lou Ann B.

If you miss calling in or submitting a urine sample, you are automatically considered dirty.

If an uncalibrated, untested breathalyzer indicates you have been drinking (a legal right denied drug court participants) you are jailed without any chance of appeal until the test comes back days or weeks later.

If you drink water and have pale urine instead of the dark, yellow urine you are accused of "diluting your urine" and threatened with imprisonment.

And heaven help you if you talk back. Only a fool would do that.

The power of the court to whimsically bestow rewards and sanctions on a drug court participant isn't just annoying, it can be disastrous. We would see this scenario play out over and over again over the course of my husband's stint in drug court. Individuals lost their jobs due to improperly calibrated breathalyzers, hearsay, and unadulterated hubris. It was far easier to point the finger at the participant and call them the loser, the liar, the failure, rather than acknowledge their own pathetic shortcomings and mistakes.

<u>Drug Courts Limit Access to Proven Treatments and Beyond</u>

The report set its sights on the drug court's approach to methadone and other non-addictive treatments: "Despite endorsements by Centers for Disease Control and Prevention, the Institute of Medicine, SAMHSA, the National Institute on Alcohol Abuse and Alcoholism, the National Institute on Drug Abuse, the World Health Organization, and even the National Association of Drug Court Professionals, many, and perhaps most, drug courts continue to prohibit methadone treatment or other maintenance therapies because of an ideological preference for abstinence."

But it doesn't stop there. Most drug courts expand their reach to other legal drugs as well, including banning drugs that treat ADD, ADHD, and even insist that participants *not* be allowed pain medication in cases where they have broken a bone or needed surgery.

Phase Three

Day 214 – 3/15/2010
Color: Green

Dave's up-level to Level Three was confirmed during his weekly counseling session and he was allowed to leave and head home. From this point forward he would only have to attend Wednesday evenings from 6-8 p.m. until the end of the program. What a relief! He finally had most of his weeks free!

Day 216 – 3/17/2010
Color: Blue and Phase Four

P.E. was sick with fever, allergies or cold, and a urinary tract infection. We missed our family counseling appointment as a result. I was two days late, took a pregnancy test, and found out we were expecting. This was unplanned, to say the least. We were both struggling to figure out what to do since I had recently lost nearly $800 in monthly income – no more office job.

Day 221 – 3/22/2010
Color: No Action

With the baby on the way and our finances in horrible shape we took P.E. out of daycare completely. This meant a savings of close to $400 per month. I emailed all of my existing clients, informed them that I was expecting Child #3 in late November, that I would be doing cleanings until mid-October, and asked if it would be all right to bring P.E. to the cleanings with me. Taking her with us would probably not start right away, but it meant that I would handle most cleanings by myself until Dave found full-time work.

Day 223 – 3/23/2010
Color: Yellow and Phase Four

We met again with Labels for our family counseling appointment. She asked, "So how are you doing with all this?" She was referring to the pregnancy and I told her, "Well, we hadn't really planned it, but we will make do." Throughout the course of our interactions together I could see her probing for a weakness, a hook, a disagreement between Dave and me, hoping for some opportunity to sink her teeth into us and pick us apart – and then undoubtedly report it to the judge and drug court team. It was exhausting to be around her, even for one short hour. I trusted her as far as I could drop-kick her. It was a relief, however, when she moved us to every other week. It was an improvement, but I was damned and determined to not tell her anything of value. I trusted a snake in the grass more than her.

Day 224 – 3/24/2010
Color: Orange and Yellow
Dave went to a training meeting with Eco-Energia. It was for a sales job, strictly commission. I was scared to death about it. 100% commission? On green energy sales in our economic downturn? It was scary to think about, and I felt like screaming at him and saying, "We can't afford for you to fuck this up!" Instead, I said nothing.

Day 235 – 4/4/2010
Color: Yellow and Blue
Dave's probation officer Sherrie heard all about Dave's new work with Eco-Energia and seemed very supportive. She suggested he speak with Lieutenant Large on Friday and see about securing some geothermal and solar installations with the Justice Center or other government offices in Harrisonville.

Day 242 – 4/11/2010

Color: Orange and Phase Four

Dave paid $100 in cash to the court for court fees. Drug court is a program that the offenders partially pay for. Different phases cost a different weekly fee, and by the time they reach Phase Four, drug court participants have usually paid out at least $1,700.

He was given a printout accounting for the fees to date that made absolutely no sense. The court clerk, a pet of the judge, refused to speak with him, saying she was busy. She then returned to talking to a co-worker about her day. Despite repeated requests, we could not get an adequate explanation of what fees are owed and how they were billed out and when. I considered writing a letter of complaint to the judge.

Day 243 – 4/12/2010

Color: Orange

Dave received a text message from Sherrie demanding he provide paycheck stubs from Mid-Continent Public Library and Cradle of Love showing that he is earning some money. He has none of these since a) he is not an employee and b) the payments have not come in yet. This would also be a cause for concern with the Eco-Energia income since he was not an employee but an independent contractor and on 100% commission.

It was an unending source of frustration since we have explained more than once that Dave is not an employee ... anywhere. For those who know of no other life than that of wage earning and paycheck collecting, the concept of business ownership or independent contractor status is foreign. It was like educating the great unwashed on how to use soap.

Day 244 – 4/13/2010
Color: Orange and Green

I wrote a letter to the judge this evening and gave it to Dave to look over.

Your Honor:

I have become increasingly frustrated by the lack of explanation of the accounting for the fees that my husband is responsible for as a participant in Cass County Drug Court.

It is very important to us to pay all of our bills promptly, but this is difficult when we do not have an accurate balance or any explanation of what the charges entail. I am responsible for all bill paying, household, and business finances and I am terribly frustrated by the lack of information or willingness for any clerk to give us an explanation of what the charges are for or what dates they cover.

I have attached a simple spreadsheet that I prepared in Excel since I needed some way of accounting for the charges and tracking our current balance. According to the information in the drug court handbook and my estimate of dates (I simply listed the charges as incurred on Mondays, the 1st work day of each week) I believe that we should currently have a credit of $5.00 (we paid $100 in cash on 4/12/10). The printout we received from the financial office does not show this and no one in the office is willing to take the time to explain how the charges (and payments) are applied. We have asked several times. The last time a clerk refused us, saying she didn't have time to explain, she then returned to a personal conversation about her day with another co-worker. It was frustrating for my husband and made me quite resentful. We want to pay this, but we need to understand what and when we are paying for.

With due consideration of the fact that at least one participant was held back from up-phasing due to a balance owed, I am sure you can understand why I am determined to pay our balance in full each month in order to avoid this situation happening to Dave. I *cannot understand why it continues to be such an issue or why the accounting of how the drug court fees are applied is done in such a hit or miss fashion.*

Please forgive me if I have overstepped my bounds. But it seems unfair to expect payment in full (zero balances) when a simple spreadsheet is completely lacking from the court and no one is willing to be accountable or explain how and when the charges/payments are applied. I appreciate any help or guidance you can give in this matter.

Dave read it over and looked at me with dread. "Please don't send this; I'm afraid they would put me in jail." He went on to explain that he had heard that the judge's pet clerk, Candy Joe, had complained about someone so vehemently that he was jailed for no other reason than because he had offended her. I set the letter aside and ended up never sending it.

Day 245 – 4/14/2012
Color: Yellow and Green
Disaster and even more threats …
Dave looked furious when he returned from submitting a UA. "I truly loathe these people." He had spoken with Sherrie and was told in no uncertain terms that he must

provide paycheck stubs for all work he "claimed that [he] was doing."

This included the Tai Chi classes, the classes he co-taught with me for Mid-Continent Public Library, and Eco-Energia. Even after any sales with Eco-Energia, she informed him that they still would not accept it since the paychecks did not list how many hours he worked. Sherrie advised him to find full-time employment (no other type of employment would be accepted) immediately or face having to serve 40 hours of community service per week until he finds approved employment.

She also said that any work he does for my cleaning biz would not count because he was not being paid directly for the work. The checks are made out to C's Cleaning Services and the net income went straight into our family accounts.

Sherrie also insisted that she had to speak with Dave's boss Tony with Eco-Energia. This of course meant that he would have to tell Tony about being in a drug court program, something we are still very close-mouthed about even in the presence of family and neighbors.

Dave went out, gathered more contacts and cards and then returned home to make the dreaded call. Moments later the change in his tone set all my fears to the side. Tony had experience with the court system and understood exactly what the probation officer needed as far as an explanation of the job, verification that Dave was working, and had provided this very same kind of job verification for another salesman with the company. "How long have you been clean and how long do you have left in the program?" Tony asked.

"I've been drug-free for 18 months and I haven't had a drop of alcohol in nine months." Dave answered.

"Don't worry about it. Not one bit," Tony reassured him, "I'll call your probation officer today and verify your employment and help her understand that even though you are on commission, you are employed."

Day 256 – 4/25/2010
Color: Yellow and Phase Four

We discovered that the baby had no heartbeat and had ceased development. We were both devastated by the news.

Day 257 – 4/26/2010
Color: Green

We were both still reeling from the news that we miscarried. We dealt with it in our different ways, and those ways seemed to change by the hour.

By late evening, our nerves were frayed. As we drove home, Dave snapped at me when I reminded him to "stay professional" after he ranted about one of the engineers. He was chomping at the bit for the guy to finish drawing up the scope of work for a potential sale. "You know, Dave, you can let me know if you are just looking for a 'yes, dear' and I'll be fine with saying that." I held myself back from adding, "I can do stupid; it's not a problem."

It was hard, so very hard. I dreaded our next therapy session, just one week away. I knew I wouldn't do anything stupid and smart off at her or share my low opinion of her counseling skills, but the last thing I wanted to do was talk about my feelings.

I wished that I could say to her, "This is where I draw the line. Drug court might be able to mandate these meetings and mandate my cooperation (with the very real threat of either separating our family unit or incarcerating my husband), but neither drug court nor you are allowed in this realm. I will not share with you these feelings because you are not a counselor I would *ever* choose willingly. This is a grief I will experience and work through on my own and with my family. It does not involve you."

I envisioned her pressing me for my feelings and asking me how I'm coping and me saying to her, "This is none of your business. I may have to speak with you, but I do not have to speak about our miscarriage. It's none of your business and, frankly, you are the last person in the world I would share my emotions with on this subject. A complete stranger would be more preferable to the pitiful excuse for a counselor that you pretend to be."

Somehow, I hoped to find a politely worded, couched in vague language, way to suggest that she fuck off and die. She was not a person I trusted or even liked. Not in the least. The thought of sharing my pain with her made my stomach turn.

Day 258 – 4/27/2010
Color: Green and Blue

Dave had spoken with Sherrie the day before regarding his current work activities. He described the sales jobs he is currently working on procuring and she asked for a simple report detailing how he has spent his hours last week, this week, and next week. She said she would copy the drug court team on this and opined that it would be satisfactory for now.

Several drug court participants were currently in jail, one for not remembering to call/drop, one for forging documents, and the other for "criminal behavior." Would it be too much to hope that with everyone else screwing up, the drug court team would step back from their over-zealous scrutiny of us? When I asked that out loud Dave just laughed bitterly. "Not a chance," he said, "If anything, it will get worse."

Day 259 – 4/28/2010

Color: Green and Blue

As Dave was getting ready to leave for a meeting, he related his Monday one-on-one counseling session with Labels to me. "Labels asked again about our hectic schedule and suggested that, with so much to do; it could increase pressure on me significantly and threaten a relapse into drugs or drinking."

He continued, "I explained that hectic did not mean chaotic. With chaos you get bad stress and the tendency to relapse. I told her that we have clear, definable goals for each day and that we discuss what needs to be done, what can wait, and areas of urgency. Each day is a steady progression toward achieving our goals of financial, emotional and physical stability. When I was done, and signing the sheet acknowledging the meeting, she had circled the 'low probability for relapse' box."

I rolled my eyes, "Yeah, just wait until she hears about the miscarriage; you will be having the discussion all over again!"

An all-day conference on green energy was cut short so that Dave could go and submit a UA in Harrisonville before 5 p.m. When he called first thing in the morning to ask if he could drop after 5 p.m. in Harrisonville so that he didn't have to miss any time at the conference Sherrie admonished him, "You didn't give me any notice. That's criminal thinking to expect we can simply accommodate you with no notice." It was criminal thinking to ask if he can drop within one hour of the cut-off. Really?

I bit my tongue but couldn't hold back from asking, "I wonder if being a heinous bitch comes naturally to her or if she has to work at it."

Day 266 – 5/5/2010
Color: Orange and Blue

Court was held a day early due to it being Mother's Day weekend.

Sherrie had requested an accounting of Dave's week, which he delivered yesterday, including a list of contacts, in order to show the drug court team what he is working on and the hours in a day/week that he is busy. We hoped they would then allow him to continue working without interference.

Due to my miscarriage he listed himself as doing all of the cleanings for the past two weeks. Sherrie noticed this and requested copies of checks, which I glared at him rebelliously over after he relayed the message.

"I don't like it either," he said, "It's none of their business how much money you make, but since I'm listed as having done the work, they want to know how much."

She glanced at the pages of contacts, about 25 in all, and along with a thorough list of his daily activities seemed satisfied.

"This is impressive," she said as she looked things over, "We probably won't even get to talking about you until next week, however, since we currently have three participants in jail at the moment."

Dave looked stunned, "Three? THREE? Wait, there's Little Girl, Beer Brat, and who else?"

"You'll see in the morning; they'll be wearing orange." She turned back to the list of contacts. "So, if we contacted some of these people, what would they say?"

"They would say that yes, they had talked to me about geothermal or solar applications for their homes or businesses."

Dave hesitated and then said, "If you must call them, please don't call them all. Whoever you do contact, once you tell them you are my probation officer in drug court, that person is not going to do business with me. I understand you may have to contact some of them, but for each one you do, that's a sale I most certainly *won't* be making."

This was the ultimate catch-22. The probation officers were notorious for setting up parolees or drug court participants in untenable positions ... you are required to get a job. Okay, now that you have a job, they need to verify you have a job and that means calling your boss. No matter how well-behaved an employee is, when the employer gets a call from their employee's PO it is unnerving at the very least.

At the worst it sets the wrong tone for the work relationship. Suddenly, the employer has unprecedented power to hire, fire, or otherwise abuse the employee/felon. "Do [fill in the blank] or I'll tell your PO. Keep your mouth shut or I'll fire you and then you'll end up with a parole violation because I know you have to keep a job to stay out of jail."

The system is broken. And here we were, stuck inside, with no power to fix it.

There was a positive aspect for the week- the three drug court participants currently in jail. It wasn't positive for them obviously, but all I could think of was that anything that kept the team's attention off of us was good. If the others tripped up and made foolish mistakes it, a) made us look better and, b) kept the drug court team's hands full of dealing with them.

We wanted to blend into the woodwork and have everyone just pass us by. We weren't doing anything wrong, but when things were quiet, the drug court team seemed to have nothing better to do with their time than pick on us. It was incredibly frustrating and stressful when they did. We struggled to make ends meet, ran from appointment to cleaning to class, and tried to keep our life as normal as possible each day. When the team had a few quiet weeks, they turned on the non-troublemakers with a vengeance, sure that we were up to no good and would stress out our already fragile little world.

Day 267 – 5/6/2010
Color: Orange

In court the drug court officers questioned Dave in detail about his work with Eco-Energia. There were rapid-fire questions all around. By the end of it they seemed satisfied that yes, he was working for this company and yes, he did know a lot about what he was selling. I hoped they would back off a little about needing an accounting of hours from him each week.

Day 269 – 5/9/2010 - Mother's Day
Color: Green

We went to Pierpont's for Mother's Day brunch and Dave took a long, slow look around. "Go ahead and have your mimosa," he advised. I looked around as well, just as paranoid.

"Are you sure? Because if you are nervous about it, just tell me. I don't need to have one."

"Go ahead; it will be fine."

After Phase One of drug court was complete, Dave was allowed to go into restaurants again, but he was still not allowed to be at a table where alcohol was being served. No matter that he was not drinking, if a drug court official saw him at a table with alcohol on it, he would be in jail for 36 hours before he had time to explain.

Even being able to pass a Breathalyzer would have no effect – they would consider him to be associating with someone who was abusing alcohol. You can believe he was damned sure there wasn't anyone he knew around before he made that decision!

The brunch was fabulous ... and so was the mimosa.

Day 275 – 5/15/2010 - Garden Party
Color: Blue

Shortly before our house/garden party started at 2 p.m., Dave received a phone call from one of the drug court participants. Dynamite had been scheduled to work at a recycling event that day for several hours as required for his mandatory community service. He showed up and no one was there. He called Sherrie, no answer, so then he called Dave.

It was dreary and rainy and cold. "No man, I haven't heard anything about it being cancelled," Dave replied on the phone.

Dynamite finally heard back from Sherrie who simply said, "Well, you'll just have to make up the hours some other time."

No explanation, no particular concern, although she is the coordinator in charge of setting up when they do community service or not.

Dave learned on Monday that the same thing happened to another guy later Saturday and then two or three more drug court participants on Sunday. The event had apparently been cancelled, but Sherrie never bothered to call and tell them.

This all had such a familiar ring to it. Again and again the drug court participants are told covertly or overtly that their time is unimportant, their needs in regard to family or employment irrelevant, and their futures doomed to a cycle of repetitive failures and drug use. They are told they are not trusted and are, quite frankly, untrustworthy.

They are accused of lying when often they have not; they are ridiculed whenever they dare to aspire to better than what the drug court officers believe to be their lot in life.

This is dark territory to walk into. Labels have a terrible way of being proven true. If you tell a child he is stupid enough times, he believes it. This doesn't suddenly change with adulthood, especially if that person's childhood was damaged with drugs or abuse. Many of these participants are developmentally behind for a variety of reasons – drugs, neglect, and more.

Many of them are like Little Girl, who at 20 is still the mental age of a 12-year-old in many respects due to her drug use (mainlining meth for the first time at 12 years of age). Is it any wonder so many of these participants fail repeatedly to turn their lives around?

Day 284 – 5/24/2010

Color: Blue and Phase Four

Mondays are Dave's one-on-one meeting with Labels. Close to the end of the session she told him that they would not meet the following week due to it being Memorial Day. He made a note on his calendar and said, "Wow, 376 days."

"376 days for what?" Labels asked.

"Since I have had any alcohol or drugs in my system," he replied.

Her mood turned sour, "So you aren't taking your sobriety day by day?"

Dave was confused, "Of course I am, but every time I go to court the judge asks "how many days" and I give her that number."

Labels still looked sour. "So, what you are telling me is that you aren't concerned about your sobriety on a daily basis. What would your sponsor think of that?"

Dave wasn't sure what to say to her. It felt like she had to come up with something to fix about him and that this insignificant thing was the best she could do.

I despised the woman. Her face showed everything-and usually it was insulting. When we discussed the classes that we teach, there was a sneer of derision. I half expected her to slip up someday and say out loud, "Really, a couple of pathetic druggies teaching classes? As if anyone should be listening to you."

When P.E. would misbehave in even the slightest way Labels would roll her eyes or put on a moronic "I'm so shocked" expression. I could not figure out if the woman was completely dismissive of our accomplishments or so resentful and jealous, she could not stand it. Either way, she was where she was because of a complete lack of ability on her part. No one in their right mind would hire her as a therapist. Unfortunately, that meant we were stuck with her. I pity those who have followed us in the years since.

Day 286 – 5/26/2010
Color: Yellow and Green

After finishing our morning cleaning, we stopped back at home to eat lunch. Dave called the probation office in Belton to ensure there was someone there who could do the UA and we headed there as soon as we were done eating. P.E. and I waited in the car while he went inside.

"Oh my God, that was the worst experience ever!" he said as he slid into his seat and we drove away. He related it to me as we drove to the next cleaning.

It had started fine enough. The officer inside was someone he had dealt with in the past and he greeted Dave with a friendly enough manner. Once the urine was in the cup and the test strip was read, his demeanor changed drastically.

"Mr. Shuck," he said sternly, "what was your drug of choice?"

"Marijuana."

"What *else*, Mr. Shuck?"

"Um, alcohol?" Dave was confused by the man's reaction and concerned.

The officer looked frustrated and pissed off, "What other *illegal drugs,* Mr. Shuck?"

"None." Dave's fear was mounting; what could possibly be showing up on the test strip?

"Nothing? Oh, really?" The man's voice held contempt.

"Sir, could you please be more specific? What is it you are asking me?"

"You are testing positive for cocaine, Mr. Shuck."

"No, no that is not possible. I've never done cocaine in my life." Full panic was running through Dave now.

The officer peered at the test strip. "Well, maybe I should get my glasses and look again. But if you are lying, and if this strip is correct, then you are going to jail today, Mr. Shuck."

Rapid heartbeat, sweating palms, Dave was on the verge of a panic attack. "Please could we get someone else in here to look at it?"

A few tense moments later another officer appeared. Unfamiliar with the test strip he needed assistance deciphering it. The two officers discussed it for a moment and the first officer asked him how many lines he saw next to cocaine. "Two." The second officer replied. This indicated a negative for cocaine. "But that second line isn't as dark as I would like it to be." He stared over at Dave.

Dave shook his head, "They about gave me a heart attack."

"For Christ's sake! Who in the hell tries to read a test strip without their glasses? What kind of incompetent morons work there?" I was pissed. "And what was up with that last comment? Negative means negative! Do they have a high school education? Can they add? How stupid are they?"

There was of course no apology. Drug court officials, probation officers, judges, and all the rest of their ilk seem to share one common trait – they view all citizens as either active criminals or future criminals. Since Dave has 'proven' himself a criminal in their eyes, they can imagine no other world in which he might be something more or different. Therefore, why would he even *deserve* an apology?

Day 302 – 6/11/2010
Color: Yellow

Our lawyer from a civil case we filed in California called. She had spoken to the judge and was calling Dave to let him know she needed him in California on July 13th and 14th to submit to a doctor's examination and give his deposition. The judge's office ok'd the trip and gave Dave a window of the 12th through the 15th for travel time. It seemed that all of his good behavior was paying off.

The defense would pay for the trip since they were requiring this extra trip to be made. Both Dave and I would have to return to California on August 9th for pre-trial mediation. But the trip in July would be solely Dave's.

Day 312 – 6/21/2010

Color: Orange and Green

I had a thumping migraine after two full cleanings and being outside in the 100+ degree heat and Dave chaired an NA meeting on Fridays from 6:30 to 7:30. He returned late, frustrated with one of the members who stuck around talking his ear off after the meeting was over. Dave had originally been rather impressed with this guy, as he seemed educated and intelligent, and Dave had initially asked him to be his sponsor. He had declined, telling Dave that he had a long way to go before he would be a good sponsor.

After knowing him for nearly a year, Dave's opinion of him had dropped considerably. The guy left his wife and two kids, stating he wanted a divorce. When he realized he might actually have to pay child support and possibly alimony, he moved back in, saying he wanted to work things out.

By this time his wife, who had been opposed to divorce for so long despite his verbal abuse, had grown a spine and realized she deserved better. So now she was asking for a divorce and he was whining about how he was trying to "work it out for the family's sake."

This saga, as well as the many details of the situation which I won't go into here, had Dave gritting his teeth. He was disgusted with the guy and shocked at his narcissism and immaturity. It also served as a reminder to me of how dedicated Dave was to me and P.E.

Day 313 – 6/22/2010
Color: Orange and Green

The night before, Dave's NA sponsor announced that he had relapsed. Dave immediately worried that the news would filter back to treatment and the drug court team. According to the rules, if your sponsor relapses, you need to find a new sponsor. He didn't exactly have a lot of choices to pick from. So instead he decided to say nothing until he could locate another sponsor and hope that no one else found out.

The next day Swimmer would graduate. Considered by most to be the shining star of drug court, the golden boy if you will, his departure from the program would mean that Dave was now the best performer there. In fact, when Dave dropped off his paperwork to Sherrie, she made mention of it. She told him that almost everyone was pleased with his progress.

The probability of Dave being phased up to Phase Four (the final phase of the drug court program) had been mentioned repeatedly by Sherrie and others. We are crossing our fingers that this happens on July 2nd. It will be our fourth wedding anniversary on that day.

Day 316 – 6/25/2010
Color: Green and Phase Four
Budget cuts in the county had impacted Sherrie's availability on Fridays. She was no longer available to supervise UAs at the Probation and Parole office on Fridays. The other workers at the office, which was located in Belton, had complained that it was too much work for them to supervise UAs at any time and that meant that if Sherrie was unavailable (she was now unavailable from noon to 1pm on Mondays through Thursdays) or absent, the drug court participant would have to drive the 26 miles south to Harrisonville and go to treatment or the county jail to submit to a Breathalyzer and UA when their color came up.
Day 316 was a Friday and Dave's color, so he drove to Harrisonville and went first to treatment, per protocol. They told him that he should go to Probation and Parole, and he reminded them of Sherrie's absence there.

"Well, you'll have to go to the jail because James isn't here to supervise a UA." UAs are typically supervised by same gender and opposite genders are not allowed to conduct one – the exception to this was Sherrie.

So, Dave drove to the jail where they promptly balked again saying they didn't have time to do a Breathalyzer and UA. When Dave explained the reason, he couldn't go to the other two locations, the officer let him in and then announced, "Well, we don't have any Breathalyzer tips." He looked at Dave, shrugged, and said, "I guess we'll just have to keep you here until we do."

"When will that be?" Dave asked.

"Monday."

"Wait a minute, you want to keep me here until Monday to take a Breathalyzer test because you don't have any Breathalyzer tips?" Dave was inside the jail at this point with no way to get out.

"Yeah, sure, why not?"

Dave began to panic, "Look, could you call Officer Crane or Deputy Good Ole Boy or Lieutenant Large and ask about this, please?"

The officer shrugged and called Deputy Good Ole Boy, who promptly advised him to collect the UA sample and let Dave be on his way.

I'm not sure which makes me more furious; the lack of clear protocol, or the complete disregard for the individual.

This common theme kept running in the background throughout our drug court experience and it was loud and clear: *You aren't entitled to basic respect or understanding. You are just some fucked-up druggie who deserves contempt and no level of respect. Your time and family and commitments are unimportant, your life is unimportant. Complain and we will punish you. Deviate from our schizophrenic commands and we will punish you.*

Is this where our justice system is at? If someone breaks the law, are they entitled to no basic human respect at all? Who are these so-called justice officials? Bullies and braggarts?

Day 319 – 6/28/2010
Color: Blue and Green

Day 319 was Dave's first of two days of tryouts for the free weatherization program he was hoping to take from mid-July through late August. As soon as he arrived at the training he called in for his color and then called Sherrie to ask for her advice. He knew that he would be in training until 4:00 and wasn't sure if he needed to drive like a demon down to Harrisonville to submit a UA before 5 p.m. or what.

She seemed irritated, "Why didn't you tell me about this?"

"I did tell you, over two weeks ago."

"Well, you should have thought about this and come up with some possible solutions."

"I asked you what you thought I should do and you said 'We'll work something out.'" Dave replied, staying as calm as possible.

"Well, whatever. It's your problem. I guess you'll just need to drive down to Harrisonville each morning and call in for your color. If it's your color then you can drop and then head into the city after that."

Harrisonville was a 26-mile drive in the opposite direction.

Day 322 – 7/1/2010
Color: Blue

Dave dropped off the information Sherrie had requested on the weatherization certification training, the student grants (federal and state), and information on the HVAC program at the local community college he was enrolled in for fall. While he was there, he mentioned the possibility of being phased up to Phase Four the next day.

"You've only been at Phase Three for four months," Sherrie replied. "You aren't eligible."

Dave reminded her that he had spent an extra two weeks in the program in Phase One and that ever since, various members of the drug court had suggested he might be phased early. "It didn't happen in Phase One, or in Phase Two, so I was hoping..." he let his words trail off.

"Oh, that's right!" Sherrie had obviously forgotten talking with him just nine days earlier about the subject, "We've been promising you that and not done it. Well fine, you've got my vote."

Day 323 – 7/2/2010 - 4th Wedding Anniversary & Phase Four!

Color: Yellow

Court day. We were on such pins and needles about it that I actually forgot it was our wedding anniversary until my dad called mid-morning to wish us a happy anniversary.

Success! Dave was elevated to Phase Four and everyone seemed very pleased with him. The judge was playful, teasing him as she reviewed his paperwork, saying, "Now let me think, is there something else we need to discuss with you, Mr. Shuck?"

Dave smiled, "Yes, your honor, I wanted to thank you for believing in me enough to allow me to go to California for four days. I really appreciate it and I won't disappoint you."

"We know you won't, Mr. Shuck, and we do believe in you. That's why we are going to go ahead and phase you up to Phase Four today."

Having been so sure and then horribly disappointed, I wasn't willing to believe it until he came home and gave me the good news. This meant he only had to attend one NA meeting per week, his one-on-one meetings with Labels were reduced to once every second week, and our couples counseling appointments re reduced to once per month.

Best yet, this is the final phase of drug court. It had been nearly a full year and we finally found ourselves in the home stretch. The end is in sight.

The Bigger Picture

By now I've spoken a lot about the drawbacks and our frustrations as we made our way through drug court. Don't let that fool you, because I am an advocate of drug diversion as an alternative to incarceration. On every level, drug diversion programs are preferable to locking people up.

However, there are several inconsistencies that affect drug court programs, at least the one I've had experience with, that truly need remedying.

Replace Drug Court with Care and Counseling

After studying drug court from within and without, I have to agree with the Drug Policy Alliance and say that they are *not* the answer to our problem.

We need to stop treating drug addiction as a crime and instead as a disease. This requires changing our laws, legalizing (or at the very least decriminalizing them) and instead moving even a portion of the billions we are spending on the War on Drugs to providing counseling and rehabilitation to addicts.

According to the National Institute for Drug Abuse, the principles for effective treatment include:

- Addiction is a complex but treatable disease that affects brain function and behavior.
- No single treatment is right for everyone.
- People need to have quick access to treatment.
- Effective treatment addresses all of the patient's needs, not just his or her drug use.
- Staying in treatment long enough is critical.
- Counseling and other behavioral therapies are the most commonly used forms of treatment.
- Medications are often an important part of treatment, especially when combined with behavioral therapies.

- Treatment plans must be reviewed often and modified to fit the patient's changing needs.
- Treatment should address other possible mental disorders.
- Medically assisted detoxification is only the first stage of treatment.
- Treatment doesn't need to be voluntary to be effective.
- Drug use during treatment must be monitored continuously.

Increase Funding for Mental Health Services

According to ElevationsHealth[24] 2016 article *The Annual Cost of the War on Drugs*, the United States government has spent over $1 trillion fighting the war on drugs. "In 2015 alone $36 billion was spent on the war on drugs, but that number was just for law enforcement and some social services, and does not take into account the cost of incarceration for nonviolent drug offenders once they are arrested and sentenced to jail."

The article goes on to say that "Roughly $80 billion is spent each year on incarcerating American prisoners and since 50% of our prison population is serving time for drug-related crimes that means that an additional $40 billion needs to be added to $36 billion price tag for the war on drugs, bringing the grand total to $76 billion."

What if we spent just half of that amount on mental health services and rehabilitation for drug addicts? What would that look like? Through a combination of behavioral therapy, small group and one-on-one counseling that was positive and empowering in nature (instead of threatening with incarceration) we could make a difference in the lives of people who are using drugs to cope with depression, physical and mental illness and pain.

Increase Education

Knowledge is power. How often have you heard that? With it, we can change our lives. Become *more* than we currently are. For many, the education in their youth was sketchy. Perhaps they didn't do well in school. Perhaps their home life was lacking. And many of these participants are parents themselves. Drug court offered many mini-programs already, but with increased funding these programs could be expanded to include:

- Parenting classes
- Personal communications/relations classes
- Nutrition, health, and meal preparation

- Job skills (computer literacy, typing, skills assessment, exposure to different work environments)
- Self-sufficiency, DIY, crafts – even entrepreneurship

Yes, nearly all of these are offered to one extent or another already. What I am suggesting is a far more intensive program, one that encourages and promotes a different lifestyle, one filled with confidence, direction, and purpose.

<u>Change the Message</u>

This message that we experienced over and over- "you are an addict; you are lost to your addiction"-can be counter-productive. Instead of tearing an individual down, with the intent of then rebuilding them into a better design, perhaps we should be focusing on empowering the individuals with hope, belief, and dedication.

They absolutely *can* live productive, drug-free lives. That should be the message- quickly followed by real examples that are *within their grasp*. Over and over during our experience in drug court we were presented with the unspoken message: *Conform to our expectations of what you should be.* Apparently, those expectations included a paycheck-McDonald's or Sonic was perfectly acceptable-and *not* a business of our own or an atypical job of any kind. Instead of lauding my husband's efforts to start his own martial arts business, the judge publicly ripped up his business plan, tossing it onto the ground. It was devastating.

The message must be changed to:
- You absolutely can change your life and we are here to help you do that
- You have a mind and a heart – feed it, embrace life and opportunities
- Do not place limits on your own capabilities
- Believe in yourself

It may be Pollyanna of me to believe that this approach could be more effective than the carrot and the stick, but there you go. I never liked the carrot and the stick approach. I was always tempted to rip the stick out of someone's hand, beat them with it, and then shove that damned carrot down *their* throat.

Each of us has such amazing potential – even those who were stunted by drugs like Little Girl or Beer Brat. Each of them still has the capacity for great things – even small things – like living a drug-free life. We shouldn't be telling people what they *can't* do or are *incapable* of. We shouldn't be limiting their dreams. We should be replacing their addictions with the reality of who they are inside and the potential of what wonderful opportunities they have for their lives. Change the message and you may very well change the outcome.

Avoid the Incarceration/Punishment Model

When you are there in the thick of it, fighting the good fight, trying to save people from themselves, it is easy to lose perspective. It's easy to get frustrated, to develop calluses and thick skin-you have heard every lie in the book, after all.

The drug court officers may be good people, they may have their hearts in the right place, but in the end, they are still approaching this from an incarceration/punishment model. To even think of issuing some kind of retribution on a person for speaking his mind (something you will read about in the next chapter) speaks volumes to *where* these individuals are coming from. They *say* it isn't about incarceration, retribution or punishment, but their *actions* and *responses* clearly demonstrate that it is.

It is especially easy to fall into this trap of punishment versus rehabilitation when you consider who the drug court officers are. They are judges, police officers, and prosecutors. No matter how good their intentions are, their training and experiences dictate reality. They still see the drug court participants as criminals and drug addicts. To some level they still rationalize it all by thinking, and often saying, "They should just be thankful they aren't in prison right now."

Perhaps it is our cultural perception at work here, but incarceration is *never* the answer to drug addiction. If anything, it makes the disease worse and commits an individual to a lifetime sentence as a convicted felon, one who is stripped of opportunities and options.

Often the drug court team's actions were not proactive, but rather reactive. This is understandable in the sense that you can't be prepared for every possibility, every outcome, but reaction must be carefully tempered with discussion, time, and thought. How will the reaction affect the drug court participants? Will it provide a necessary learning opportunity? Is it vindictive, borne out of frustration at an individual participant?

And lastly, the fact that accusations, rudeness, and disrespect were dished out as a weekly, even daily, occurrence – without any thought to apology or recognition that what they were doing was unfair, unkind and just plain *wrong* – was reprehensible. It was a constant reminder that we were nothing better than misbehaving children without any rights to an apology when they were in the wrong.

All you accomplish with that behavior is to remind the drug court participant that 1) life is not fair and never will be and 2) they aren't important enough to warrant an apology when someone has wronged them (although it is certainly expected when the situation is reversed).

Improve these aspects of drug court and the recidivism rates will be blown out of the water.

Legalize Marijuana

We consume a great deal of legal drugs each day in this country – cigarettes, alcohol, chocolate, and caffeine – and all of them are far more addictive than marijuana will ever be.

According to Dr. Jann Gumbiner, author of *Is Marijuana Addictive?*[20], "Compared to other substances, marijuana is not very addicting. It is estimated that 32% of tobacco users will become addicted, 23% of heroin users, 17% of cocaine users, and 15% of alcohol users. Cocaine and heroin are more physically harmful and nicotine is much more addictive.

It is much harder to quit smoking cigarettes than it is to quit smoking pot."

So, I'll say it clearly – marijuana is *not* addictive in the traditional "I'm a drug addict" sense of the word. It just isn't. Numerous research studies back this fact up.

Mankind has used marijuana in one form or another since before recorded history. It should not be illegal, and it certainly should not be a Schedule 1 drug. We need to legalize this drug so there is no longer any more confusion – drug *treatment* should be for drug addicts (cocaine, heroin, methamphetamines, and others, *not* marijuana smokers). Adult marijuana smokers and producers should not be prosecuted – no more than cigarette smokers, tobacco producers, beer drinkers or breweries should.

This will eradicate the need for marijuana smokers and producers to, a) clog up the judicial system with unnecessary prosecution of an often harmless (and research has indicated it to be *beneficial* in some cases) drug, and, b) allow the drug treatment programs to focus on the true addicts who need help the most. It would also save our country billions of dollars in taxpayer funds for the prisons that incarcerate the non-violent users or producers, along with the many other tentacles of cost (foster care for children of marijuana smokers and producers, prosecutors, judges, and drug enforcement personnel).

Once we legalize marijuana, we can turn our attention to rehabilitation and drug treatment programs for the serious, life-destroying drugs that have been taking a backseat to marijuana in the past two decades. Once our focus is where it should be, we can actually make progress towards reducing addiction and improving lives.

Hell, Legalize EVERYTHING

While I am shaking the tree, I might as well take on the whole enchilada and suggest what might seem like a revolutionary idea – why not legalize all drugs for adult consumption? Does this seem drastic? There are several examples we can look at and see just how successful such a maneuver would be.

In *Breaking the Taboo*[21], the documentary focuses on Portugal and Switzerland, two countries with rampant drug use and, in the case of Switzerland, skyrocketing cases of HIV and heroin addiction. "In Portugal, they decided to decriminalize the use of all drugs." Individuals caught possessing drugs are not charged with a crime, they are not thrown in prison. Instead they are brought before a "dissuasion board" comprised of psychiatrists and social workers who seek to understand the needs of these people intercepted by police. They offer help – not incarceration. "The most fundamental step you need to take is to realize that addiction is a medical problem and therefore addicts need to be treated medically, not criminally. If we accept that basic principle, we overcome most of the disagreements of drug policy."

In Portugal, drug use among young people has fallen steadily each year in each drug category. It has gone from the #1 issue to the rank of #13 – because the problems associated with drug use (crime, incarceration and more) have also fallen steadily as a result in the change in overall drug policy and decision to decriminalize.

Morgan Freeman, narrator for *Breaking the Taboo,* focuses next on Switzerland, "In the 90s, Switzerland faced an AIDS epidemic rapidly spreading through the heroin-using population … As President [of Switzerland], Global Commissioner Ruth Dreifuss called for a series of dramatic solutions to the epidemic including medically prescribed clean needles and heroin to addicts who couldn't kick the habit."

Imagine that for a moment. They actually *supplied heroin* to addicts. So what was the result? According to *Breaking the Taboo*, "In Switzerland, the number of injecting drug users with HIV/AIDS has been reduced by over 50 percent in ten years."

Five Reasons to Legalize Drugs

#1 - It removes the temptation and allure

Let's face it – when someone tells you that you can't do something – do you just accept it and do what they tell you? Or do you challenge it, question their assertion, and think of ways around it?

By the end of Prohibition, there were more consumers of alcohol than there were at the beginning of it. And the War on Drugs has proved, over and over, the same situation is true.

Instead of spreading lies or misinformation ("marijuana will make you go insane!"), we should focus on the truth and stop using such simplistic messages as "just say no." It hasn't worked with teenage pregnancy and it isn't going to deter the curious from experimenting.

#2 – Legalization will destroy the illegal drug trade

The cartels' rise to power has come from the War on Drugs. Like the mythological Hydra, hack off one of their heads and two will rise in their place. It reminds me of a parenting technique I learned decades ago – when a child is spoiling for a fight, take the wind out of their sails. Don't engage. They will have nowhere to go.

If we legalize drugs we eliminate most of drug traffickers' profit. A kilo of cocaine sells for around $1,000 in Columbia – but due to its illegal nature it costs close to $100,000 on a New York street. If the profit is no longer there, the cartels will collapse.

#3 - It directs our focus to prevention, treatment, and rehabilitation

We need to stop thinking of addicts as something less than human. Ruth Dreifuss puts the question and answer eloquently, "Who are the addicts? Our children. People we love, people we would like to bring back."

We won't bring these people back by beating them over the head with a stick. We will bring them back by giving them love, some semblance of acceptance, and thereby sharing with them the hope that they can regain control of their lives.

As former President Bill Clinton says in *Breaking the Taboo*, "There should be safe places where people with addiction can come and not think they are going to be arrested. Where they can have their basic needs met. I have experience with this, including personal experience. I had a brother who was addicted to cocaine. So I know a lot about this and I understand, more than most people do, what is involved."

#4 - It reduces overall usage

Perhaps this goes hand-in-hand with #1 – but take away the allure, the romanticism of "doing something bad" and coupled with #3, you will see a dramatic drop in usage.

People respond to kindness and acceptance far better than they ever will to alienation or punishment. Legalization will reduce hard-core drug use by leaps and bounds.

#5 – It will return this nation once again to "the land of the free"

We are NOT free. Not in a nation that has over 25% of the world's total number of prisoners incarcerated within its borders. Instead we are a nation of the afraid, of the watched, and of the hunted. We have given over control of our bodies to the government – and that government seems intent on ensuring we end up incarcerated.

Something has to change – WE have to change. The tide is turning and a large wave, one that is favorable toward marijuana usage by adults, has begun to pick up speed. Two states (Washington and Colorado) have recently passed legislation legalizing marijuana, 14 have decriminalized possession of small amounts, and 18 states have passed medical marijuana bills. All of these are steps in the right direction – but the bigger problem of the War on Drugs still looms as long as other drugs remain illegal.

Phase Four

Day 324 – 7/3/2010
Color: Orange and Yellow
Today was the first day of Dave calling in as a Phase Four. From here on out, he only has to submit a UA if Phase Four is listed, not green. Hopefully this will be few and far between and not put undue pressure on him while he is in classes and training.

Day 333 – 7/12/2010
Color: Orange and Blue
Dave left on a short trip to California to submit to a doctor's examination by the defense, as well as providing his deposition. This was authorized by the drug court judge. He was scheduled to return on Thursday, Day 336.

Day 336 – 7/15/2010 - Dave's trip to California

Color: Phase Four

I mistakenly reserved Dave to return on the red eye at 1:30 a.m. California time. He returned exhausted and promptly took a four-hour nap before we had to go to the meeting with Labels. Our 'homework'-to come up with some area of our relationship that needed work-was due at the meeting. We told her we had spoken repeatedly about it and simply couldn't come up with anything.

When situations came up that we disagree on, we have learned to discuss it, and either concede or come to a compromise. Few times, if ever, have we simply not been able to agree. The only example I can come up with is our disagreement on whether to live in an old house or not. That one is easy ... eventually we will move into his parents' house after they have passed. That house was built in 1906 and definitely qualifies. And I've already told him that if I make it big as a writer, we are buying a house that I want. And that will definitely be an old house.

In any case, this stance led Labels to ask the obvious question – how will you avoid drugs in the future if you are both willing to compromise?

I reminded her that I left my first husband in no small part over his insistence on continuing to abuse drugs even at the expense of his wife and child having less to eat or a decent roof over our heads. I also reminded her that the raid had come at a moment when we were reaching a decision point. Dave had been smoking out in the garage since before P.E. was born. She had just turned two years old and was becoming more and more curious about what her Daddy was doing in the garage. I had warned Dave that he could not continue to smoke pot at the level to which he had been smoking and that something would have to change.

Dave joined in at this point and added, "I knew, because she had begun to mention it more frequently, that it was simply a matter of time before I had to stop. I didn't want to think about it, but I figured I had about two more months max before Christine put her foot down and insisted that I stop."

Day 354 – 8/2/2010
Color: Yellow and Phase Four
One of the participants scheduled to graduate in less than two weeks is in jail after an argument with his wife. Apparently, the argument grew heated, and when he tried to retreat and cool off, she followed him. He

finally slapped her and she called the police, who immediately arrested him. At this point she has declined to press charges, but the damage is already done. He has been sitting in jail for over a week now, wondering and worrying that he might be faced with his full sentence as well as domestic abuse charges.

Considering that they continue to let repeat offenders back into the program, and give them repeated chances, it is unlikely that they will kick Millionaire out of the program.

Dave mentioned that Millionaire's wife never took the program seriously and has been a hindrance from the start.

Email from Dave:

"Millionaire was in jail as of last Wednesday. He is supposed to say that he got into an argument with his wife and that he tried to leave the area. She followed him from room to room, not letting him get away to cool off. There is also some speculation that she was hitting him. He slapped her and she called the cops. She doesn't want to press charges, but it's too late. The police are pressing charges of spousal abuse.

Millionaire was supposed to graduate in 2 weeks. There is a policy that says that no one in drug court can pick up any new violent charges or they will be terminated from the program, facing the full charge and time for their crime. He is now looking at 15 years."

Day 362 – 8/10/2010
Color: Yellow and Blue

Dave received a call while in class from his P.O., "Dave, this is Sonia. I don't have any record of you dropping yesterday. Either let me know where you dropped or call me on your way to jail."

He called and left her a message that he dropped at Belton Probation and Parole.

No call back from her.

He called later to see if she got the message. "Yeah, I had to dig through all the bags of urine to find yours. Thanks. They didn't let me know that you had been in." Her attitude was that Dave had done something wrong. "Also, you need to go to community service on Saturday."

He told her that he had to teach a class on Saturday and asked why he hadn't been informed sooner.

"Well, I posted a copy at treatment in July. Millionaire was scheduled but since he can't be there, it's you. Call Allen; I will approve you switching with him."

Millionaire has been in jail for 3 weeks and this was the first we had heard of any change in schedule.

Day 363 – 8/11/2010

Color: Orange

Dave returned from his weekly Wednesday group meeting over an hour late. He was still seething when he arrived home at 9:30 that evening. He was informed that any NA or AA meetings headed by drug court members would no longer count toward the minimum number of weekly meetings he needed to attend.

The issue of meetings not being headed by drug court attendees (he was heading two per week at the time) was because the confidentiality and anonymity of the meetings had been violated – an attendee had told one of the drug court team that there were meetings that were mostly attended by drug court participants and that at least one of the meetings was only 30 minutes long. Only a small handful of meetings had gone like this – mainly due to lack of sharing by participants.

He was also informed that there would be a mandatory meeting on the following Friday with an informational documentary about the Holocaust.

As the grandson of Polish Jew (Dave's maternal grandmother) and Polish gypsy (Dave's maternal grandfather), Dave was quite well aware and informed when it came to the Holocaust. He had also had plans to be at a training hosted by Children's Mercy for the Healthy Homes program that they were rolling out. He was to be in the first group to ever be trained to do the Healthy Homes assessments.

It could have turned into a good job. Instead he would have to go to this meeting and attend a class on the Holocaust, "Taught by a goyim, who will tell me that the nasty Nazis killed a lot of people. It is a good thing for the participants to know about history, but this seems to out of the scope of Drug Court, don't you agree?"

After the group meeting was over, Dave stayed to talk to Sonia, who was one of the more reasonable drug court officers. He described the drug court team as behaving like a bunch of bullies or, even better, like a kid with a magnifying glass who wants to burn the legs off of some ants.

He recalled to her an old *Life in Hell* cartoon, where the rabbit is in a straightjacket that is chained to a chair in a padded cell. There is a small slide in the door that is open so that you can see a pair of eyes staring angrily at the rabbit. The caption reads, "The beatings will continue until morale improves."

He told her that the entire Drug Court team seemed like something out of a Kafka nightmare. Sonia responded by reminding him of an analogy he had made in the first few months of the program where he had compared drug court to the ocean. "The ocean neither loves nor hates you; it is incapable of such feelings. It's just the ocean. If you live or die, it could not care less."

Dave asked Sonia if she had read *The Old Man and The Sea*. She hadn't. He gave her a brief synopsis of the story and finished with, "Even though the sea might not care, it can sure fuck up our day from time to time."

Dave said that every time he started to feel as if the program was going well, something would happen to screw it all up again. "They go out of their way to make sure that we are scared. Fear is like a drug to them and they need to go to rehab to kick the habit."

None of them had ever heard of the Stanford Experiment[5] before Dave mentioned it. And after they did hear of it none of them thought that they could ever fall into the roles that the students had fallen into. They are blinded by their power and drunk on the fear that can generate.

Sonia didn't agree and asked for an example. Dave pointed to the situation ten months prior when he was anticipating moving from Phase One to Phase Two. After building him up, asking him if he was looking forward to up-phasing and the extra time he would have they decided to hold him back from progressing in the program so that they could see how he would react. It had felt as if the drug court team wanted to watch Dave squirm like a worm on a hook.

Dave then related to Sonia our first family counseling session where Labels had said in an offhand way that with the sweep of her pen, she could declare our home plan to be unacceptable. If she had done that, he would have been living at the jail until the drug court team inspected and approved other accommodations.

Dave told Sonia that he had been planning to be involved with the alumni program, mentoring new Drug Court participants and helping them to adjust to the new rules, but now all he wanted to do was to get away from them and never look back. Sadists like Director and others should never be given free license to disrupt people's lives, or play with their emotions and dreams like this.

As Dave said, "There is a special place in hell for them. May they go there soon."

Dave went on to tell Sonia that whenever he thinks about the big picture, he felt like Don Quixote charging at the dragons (windmills) and slowly grinding away his spirit, leaving him old, broken, and empty.

As for me, whenever I think back on all that we went through, a line from *Jurassic Park* runs through my head, "[They] were so preoccupied with whether or not they *could*, they didn't stop to think if they *should*."

It is as if the drug court participant is no longer human, no longer deserving of the same rights or even a basic sense of respect. And if they feel that way about us, why bother putting us through drug court? Why not just lock the sub-human loser up and be done with it?

Day 365 – 8/13/2010

Color: Green and Blue

Fridays are the weekly NA meetings. Dave left early to set up for the meeting as he typically does, but he had decided to have someone else chair the meeting. Since he did not know if drug court had decided to go forward with the new edict or not, he was erring on the side of caution. By not chairing the meeting he would still be able to have his attendance counted.

Little Girl arrived to tell him that she could not stay for the meeting; she was too scared to, and she explained why. She said, "The Director stood up in court today and said, 'Drug court cannot dictate which NA or AA meetings you attend. However, if you attend a certain meeting,' he paused and looked around at the drug court participants, 'and you know who you are, be aware of how this may reflect on your commitment to your recovery.'"

In essence, Director had become convinced that the Serenity Today meeting in Belton was populated mostly by drug court participants who used it as an easy way out of attending the NA/AA requirement insisted upon by drug court. This belief was reinforced when they caught Little Girl in a relationship with another drug court participant named Chris. Intimate relationships between drug court participants are prohibited, just as any kind of friendship or contact with a felon while in the program is strictly prohibited.

"I will *not* be run off from my home meeting," Dave stated, looking very angry. Little Girl is scared, as are several others, and they won't be coming to the meetings anymore."

There had also been reports that the drug court participants refused to share, just sat there in the meetings not participating and that the meetings often lasted only 30 minutes. Dave could remember one meeting where there were only three people, each of them had shared and the meeting had lasted 30 minutes. "Often, we go over, though.

Today we had three participants and the meeting went for an hour and 20 minutes!"

Day 369 – 8/17/2010
Color: No Action

Last Friday our lawyer in California had called us to let us know that a new mediation meeting had been set for our civil suit. This suit dated back to a 2007 traffic accident in California where a man who had been late getting back from lunch was busy texting on his phone and hit the car that Dave was a passenger in, destroying both cars and injuring Dave and his friend Tony. It had been one hell of a way to end our vacation there.

The meeting is mandatory and we were both required to attend in person. As with most things legal, there was little or no notice. The date was set for September 1st, and it was currently mid-August. Two weeks to get permission from the judge out here to travel, plus pay top dollar for the plane tickets. The only good news out of it was that I would get to see Danielle for her 22nd birthday and spend some time with her.

By Tuesday, the 17th of August, I was in a complete frazzle. No answer from the judge here in Missouri and prices for tickets had already risen $100 more dollars. Unsure of whether I should do it or not, I bought the tickets for all three of us. If Dave and I had to go, then so did P.E. I wasn't going to go all the way out to California and not give my mother-in-law an opportunity to see her youngest granddaughter for the first time in three years.

Day 381 – 8/29/2010
Color: Blue

Dave received an update on Millionaire ...

First, he will stay in jail until the charges of domestic violence are brought forth. If there is any time to be served, he will serve it. Once that is complete, he will serve 120 days in jail at the drug court's discretion and then enter the program from day one all over again.

When I heard this, I felt physically ill. A few months back, Beer Brat had been a Phase Two or Three, and been caught driving without a license, while hanging out with a known felon, and was captured after speeding through a crowded apartment complex with children all around. Did he get time in jail? No. He got a few weeks in there to think about it. No additional charges were brought against him and he was demoted to Phase One and started back in the program right away.

What reason would the drug court have to deal so severely with Millionaire over a relatively minor infraction?

Day 390 – 9/7/2010
Color: Yellow

P.E. and I returned from our week in California by mid-afternoon on Tuesday, September 7th. My first order of business was beginning to go through my 200+ emails and see if there were any that required immediate attention. As I paged through the emails, Dave came in and noticed that he had skipped a day in sending me the color of the day. This was our double-check and also served to keep me updated for this book.

I checked the phone logs on Vonage to see if he had made a phone call to the hotline on Sunday, the day in question. There was nothing. After six months of no sanctions, any sanctions on the books are set back to zero. This meant that instead of it being cumulative, and the third occurrence of him forgetting to call in, Dave would only spend 24 hours in jail, not 72. We looked over the schedule for the week and realized his best time to go would be directly after his evening class. So off he went to class, when he returned, he ate a little, called his P.O.

Sherrie and headed down to Harrisonville to turn himself in to the county jail there.

Day 391 – 9/8/2010
Color: Unknown (in jail for 24 hours)

Dave returned home at 10:30 p.m. on Wednesday evening. Truth be told, I think they released him one half hour shy of 24 hours, but I wasn't going to complain. He was back and for the first time had not been put in general population.

Instead they had placed him in an individual cell that contained a cot, toilet, and sink. In order to flush the toilet or use the sink, he had to press a button and then wait for the office to view him on the camera and release the controls.

He was told that if he ever heard the camera ticking, he was to turn and look toward the camera, face uncovered. The camera was covered with spit and the cell was filthy.

"I don't know how I would have handled any longer than 24 hours in there," Dave said, shaking his head, "I was starting to lose it big time. And the nightmares I had, damn."

I can't imagine what it must be like for those who are condemned to spend years or even decades inside of the walls of prisons.

Day 393 – 9/10/2010
Color: Yellow and Green

Marc Emery, the "Prince of Pot," was sentenced to five years in a federal prison. Emery is a Canadian citizen who, after a five-year long battle, found himself extradited to the United States to face charges of selling seeds to American citizens.

The news clip included a quote from the judge, "There is no question your actions were illegal and criminal and your actions ensured that others broke the law and suffered the consequences."

Dave had to make up his missed two hours from Wednesday (due to his 24 hours in jail) so he headed down to Harrisonville as soon as he had returned from getting the van worked on. A few hours later he was back, shaking his head over the ridiculous antics that the newer participants were up to.

Some of these people are not part of drug court, but a different program known as CSTAR. In both hour-long sessions, Dave listened as they described the medley of drugs (prescription and otherwise) and alcohol that they each took to get them high or calm down and focus ... usually all at once.

Only attending Wednesday evenings, a time reserved for participants in the drug court program who are in the higher phases of treatment, has provided Dave with an oasis of calm. The ones with less control over their addictions and behavior are simply not present. So, for most of the past six months, Dave has not had to see or deal with the 'rabble-rousers'. It was a bit of a shock.

Day 410 – 9/27/2010
Color: Green and Blue
Email from Dave:
Christine,

I was telling Labels about my yard. I mentioned that I have garden snakes breeding in my pond. I said that they are pretty little snakes, the longest being between 2.5 and 3 feet long. She looked horror stricken.

"What does P.E. think about them?" she asked.

"She thinks they are cool. I have told her that there are some snakes that are poisonous and that if you don't know if a snake is harmless, that you should stay away from them." I told her.

She told me that the last time she was in her basement, she was thinking about how snakes could be hiding anywhere. She has not been in her basement for months and is dreading ever going there again. When I asked her what was wrong with snakes, she replied that she wouldn't hate them so much if they hadn't chosen to not have legs. She said that snakes chase people and that they looked 'gross.'

How telling that Labels would have such issues with a harmless snake. It reminds me of a saying I once heard, "Many workers in the mental health field gravitate toward a career they themselves are often in dire need of." Counselors, psychologists, and the like are often just as messed up as their patients. And no, I don't think that makes them more effective at their job or more empathetic. I think it just makes them messed-up individuals with their own ghosts and skeletons to deal with, running away from their problems while pretending to help others.

In our family counseling meeting that day with Labels, I brought up William Randolph Hearst and Hearst Castle in San Simian California. Labels had a blank look on her face.

I tried to jog Labels' memory, by saying "You know, the guy who owned the newspapers?" Labels simply stared at me blankly.

I went on, "He owned massive tracts of forest land where the paper his newspapers were printed on. He was one of the most outspoken opponents of marijuana of his time. He had read articles on how growing hemp for paper could put the forest harvesting paper industry out of business, that hemp-derived plastics were the cheapest way to go, and that the hemp seeds could be used as both a food source and an easy way to create fuel. He was the father of yellow journalism and is partly responsible for the Spanish-American War. When one of his reporters came back to him and said that there was no reason for the Americans to attack Mexico, he was quoted as saying, 'You give me the pictures and I'll give you the war.' He was a profiteer and war criminal and one of the richest men in America." Labels had no idea who he was and looked incredulous.

How can a person who is involved daily with drug court participants not have some basic knowledge of history – and especially the history of drugs in America? Marijuana has been illegal for less than 100 years and many other drugs for far less than that.

It reminds me of the saying, "Those who do not learn from history are doomed to repeat it." If we cannot learn the lessons, or even know the basic facts of history, how can we deal effectively with the challenges of today? Yes, the world is different, but human nature remains the same.

Dave called his P.O. Sherrie to ask if he could take our daughter P.E. to a birthday party. She said no. The rules had changed, yet again, and he was informed that he needed to clear any event with her days in advance. When he came into the program, Phase Fours only needed to call and let her know where we would be. No permission was needed.

Day 412 – 9/29/2010

Color: Orange and Phase Four

Dave went to the Probation and Parole office to submit his UA, the first in over a month, and also to ask his P.O. Sherrie for permission to go to several upcoming events. She took his list and said they would need to vote on each and every item.

When she saw the Growing Mushrooms class, she shook her head and said, "Oh, we just had trouble with someone using mushrooms (obviously the psychedelic kind); there's no way they are going to okay this class."

Dave said, "This is a class on growing Shiitake mushrooms. That's like telling someone who just got busted for pot that he can't raise vegetables in his backyard." She just shrugged.

When he submitted his UA she commented, "You know, we should probably lab this; it's been a month since you dropped last. What do you think, Dave, should I lab this?"

She gave him a speculative stare. To send the test off to the lab means an even more thorough testing for drugs than the typical ten-drug strip they test the urine with in-house.

He just looked at her and said, "It's yours now; do whatever you want to with it."

His jaw was locked when he returned to the house. "She expected me to be mad because she denied my request to go to the birthday party." He snorted, "As if I was going to be all bent out of shape over that."

Day 413 – 9/30/2010
Color: Blue and Phase Four

Dave had to drop again at Probation and Parole here in town. When he arrived, Sherrie said, "The entire drug team is in an uproar after finding out you have been growing mushrooms in your house."

Dave stared at her incredulously, "White button mushrooms are *food*."

"Yes, but you didn't ask, and that makes it appear as if you were being sneaky or attempting to deceive us."

"Sherrie, there was no sneaking or deception at all. It never crossed my mind to ask permission, just as it never crossed my mind to ask the drug team for its permission on the vegetables that I grow in my back yard."

Dave explained, "There are literally *thousands* of types of mushrooms. You grow Shiitake mushrooms in wood, button mushrooms grow in dirt, and psilocybin mushrooms grow in cow shit. I'm sticking to the wood and dirt ones."

Sherrie thought about this for a moment. "Actually, your argument about what vegetables you grow is probably the most logical one I've heard. Let me talk to the team again and I'll get back to you on this." She paused for a moment and then asked, "What are you going to do if we tell you no?"

Dave shrugged, "Obviously, I'm going to do what the drug team dictates. I don't see that I have any other choice in the matter."

"Yes, but how will you *feel* about it?" she pressed.

"What does it matter how I feel? How does that have anything to do with drug court?" Dave shrugged again, "I've read the drug court manual several times and I've never seen anything that said I had to *like* what the drug court team decides. I simply need to abide by it."

Day 414 – 10/1/2010
Color: Yellow and Green

October 1st, 2010 – Outgoing California Governor Arnold Schwarzenegger signed Bill 1449, reducing possession of up to 28.5 grams of marijuana to a civil infraction. This is punishable by a maximum of a $100 fine, and there is no court appearance, no court costs and no criminal record associated with it. The following quote struck me deeply, "Gov. Schwarzenegger deserves credit for sparing the state's taxpayers the cost of prosecuting minor pot offenders," said California NORML Director Dale Gieringer, "Californians increasingly recognize that the war on marijuana is a waste of law enforcement resources."

The tide is turning. November 2nd was just 31 days away. That was when Californians would vote on whether to legalize the use of marijuana.

Day 415 – 10/2/2010
Color: Orange

None of the major news sources had *anything* on the new marijuana legislation. I had been checking *CNN, ABC News*, and our local stations for it and there was nothing listed. This was not the first time we had seen such glaring holes in coverage. As if by ignoring that it has happened and not giving it coverage, they will it into nonexistence.

It was a grim reminder of how information is controlled in the country. The propaganda machine is alive and well, and you can rest assured it is filtering and controlling exactly what information we as a nation actually receive.

Day 416 – 10/3/2010 - P.E.'s Birthday Party

Color: Yellow and Phase Four

I swear they always seem to sense when we are at our most hectic. The day of P.E.'s birthday party and it meant Dave had to drive down to Harrisonville to the county jail. When he arrived and explained why he was there, the sheriff looked exasperated, "Can't you go to treatment and submit there?"

Dave explained that treatment was closed on Sundays. The sheriff rolled his eyes, "So how many of *you people* will be coming down here today?" Dave just smiled and said he didn't really know. They were out of urine test strips, so the sheriff simply gave him a Breathalyzer and sent him on his way.

Day 428 – 10/15/2010
Color: Green and Phase Four

We had a cleaning to go to so Dave headed down to treatment, hoping to arrive at the perfect time between court and before classes to submit his UA. When he arrived Director told him, "I'm busy talking to someone right now; you will have to wait."

"No problem, take your time," Dave said and sat down to wait. Ten minutes later, Director finished talking with the individual and came out of his office.

He smirked at Dave and said, "I have to teach a class now. You really should have gotten here earlier."

Again, Dave said, "No problem, I've got a book, I'll wait." And wait he did for a full hour for Director to be done with the class and not have any other excuse.

"Does this guy wake up every morning and ask himself how he can be a bigger dick than the day before?" I asked. "Does he make a list? I can see it now, the title of it is 'General Dickery.' Tell me Dave, did he pull it out and look it over to see if he could mark anything else off the list?"

Dave shrugged, "You have to remember, Director is the guy who is convinced I've got a narcissistic, God complex. He's just trying to prove his theory right by pushing my buttons and I'm just going to keep letting him play his little mind games and not allow him to get to me. Also, it is a reminder again that my life is not in my control."

My fur was up, "What the hell is up with that, anyway? They keep pushing this point, but they don't seem to give people any hope that things will change. How does that help someone recover? How does that effect any change at all?"

Dave had no answer for me, other than to repeat that, in his case, Director was still eager to prove a narcissistic personality disorder. I had to agree that *someone* had a narcissistic personality disorder ... but it sure as hell wasn't Dave.

Day 437 – 10/24/2010

Color: Orange and Phase Four

A couple of weeks ago, Dave heard that one of the newer drug court participants had been in jail. The sequence of events went as follows...

Mark was awakened at one a.m. on a Saturday night by a tracker and given a Breathalyzer. He tested negative and returned to bed. In the morning he called in for the color of the day and heard his color. Since it was a Sunday, he had to go directly to the county jail for testing.

When Mark came in, he was tested on a new, un-calibrated Breathalyzer. It showed positive for alcohol, .02, and he was immediately jailed.

He insisted on a urinalysis, swearing he had not touched alcohol. They acceded to his request, and it was sent to a lab for urinalysis when it came up negative with the strip test. They used the Breathalyzer on him again later that day and received the same reading of .02.

Despite the fact that he had been in jail and that by then any alcohol in his system would have already metabolized. They should have suspected an equipment malfunction when the same level of reading was produced hours after incarceration.

He sat there in jail until Friday, when he went in front of the judge, who screamed at him, called him dishonest and threw him back in jail ... until the results came back from the lab later that day.

The results from the urinalysis were negative and they released him without any apology or admission of irresponsible behavior on their part. Meanwhile, he lost his job due to his absence and was now unemployed.

Dave suggested that perhaps, due to their negligence in simply assuming the new Breathalyzer had to be right, they might give him a free pass next time. The counselor, Fingers, laughed and said, "Absolutely not. It did him some good to be in jail; now he will be less arrogant."

Less arrogant? *Less arrogant?* The majority of the drug court officers are nothing less than malicious, small-minded ignorant monsters. How dare they decide someone is *arrogant*?

Day 441 – 10/28/2010
Color: Green and Blue

Dave asked about his graduation date while he was at treatment in Harrisonville. He was told that nothing had been decided upon for sure, but that they were considering the second or third Wednesday in December for his graduation.

There are three people coming up for graduation-Jennifer at the end of October, Dave at the end of November, and Allen at the end of December. Typically, graduations are grouped together, but the drug court team is considering three separate graduations.

Meanwhile, the looming election had caught our attention. California stood poised to legalize the use of marijuana in adults ages 18 and older. In honor of that, we watched *Super High Me* –comedian Doug Benson's take on Spurlock's *Super-Size Me*. Before beginning, Benson avoided alcohol and cannabis for a cleansing period, then smoked and otherwise consumed cannabis every day for 30 days in a row. According to Wikipedia:

> *"Benson took various tests to gauge his physical and mental health both before 30 days of not smoking cannabis, and after doing so for 30 days straight. Benson's physician concluded that the effects on Benson's health from his use of cannabis were generally inconsequential. The greatest changes noted were in his weight (Benson gained eight pounds during his "high" month). His sperm count actually increased,*

contrary to the expectations of medical studies. In an ESP test, it is arguable whether his results were notably better or worse because his "sober" ESP score was 1 correct guess out of 25, which can be considered unusable, his score while high was 7/25. His overall score on an SAT test increased (mostly verbal), although, it was mentioned that his mathematical skills were significantly reduced."

    I couldn't help wondering what would happen in the next few days. The November 2nd election was only four days away. Would Prop 19 pass?

    Here in Missouri, far away from the enlightened Left Coast, we found ourselves besieged by election signs as well. The one that continued to rankle me was Candy Joe, who was running for re-election as Circuit Clerk.

A pet of Judge Baker, she was in charge of keeping the books updated on what each drug court member owed. Yes, this was the same one who couldn't be bothered to update the totals on a once-monthly basis. She was also the one who told Dave she "didn't have time to talk to him" and then continued to have a conversation on what she had eaten for lunch with a co-worker while on the clock, instead of doing her job and answering his question.

When drug court participants had complained that they didn't have updated totals, she had whined to the judge that they were rude to her. In at least one case, that individual was jailed.

Was Candy Joe a servant of the people? I think not. From my perspective, it seemed that she considered the people to be her servants – especially those lowly druggies. Why would I elect her to continue to *not* do her job?

Unfortunately, her rival was fighting an uphill battle. Dave said, "I met her rival, and the woman's teeth look like they are rotting out of her head."

"Great. So … what, she's a meth head?" I asked, incredulous.

"No, no, she's far too large to be a meth head." he replied, grinning.

It was all tongue in cheek between us, but I had small hope that the rival will win. First impressions are what most people go on.

I guess if I want to be "the change I see in the world" then I will have to run for Circuit Clerk. Honestly though, who would want that job, anyway? I doubt I could tolerate being that close to Judge Baker and the rest of that group of thugs on a daily basis – no matter what they paid me.

As a note of interest – the challenger ended up winning the election, and in fall of 2013 was removed from office *with pay* while facing complaints of incompetence. Your tax dollars at work.

Day 445 – 11/1/2010
Color: Orange and Blue

Dave received his graduation paperwork from Sherrie today. He had to answer a questionnaire, and possibly write a paper on what he had learned in drug court.

Day 446 – 11/2/2010
Color: Orange and Blue

Election Day. We learned that evening that Prop 19 had failed to pass in California. We both just shrugged and said little, but it felt like another nail in the coffin. Why had it failed? Our hopes for an avalanche of legislation flooding the other states and making marijuana legal in just a few years' time were dashed.

Looking back, I would have to say that by this time, we were numb. The daily stress of drug court, even now in its less restrictive aspects, was still with us; hanging over us with everything we said or did. Just for once we wanted a "win," a big one that would boost our spirits and give us hope that others wouldn't find themselves in our situation, but the election on November 2nd, 2010 would not give us that "win" we so deeply desired.

Day 448 – 11/4/2010
Color: Blue

We had our last family counseling appointment with Labels. It was rather informal, since we were wrapping up, so I spoke about how I was participating in November's NaNoWriMo. She asked me what I was looking forward to with the drug court program ending. "More time," I said, "I'm looking forward to more time for work, family, and school."

She smiled at Dave and said, "I'll bet you'll have withdrawals, not having to call for your color each day."

We both looked at her and said, "I doubt that." Dave went on to tell her about me asking him what his color was on Tuesday, scared he had forgotten to call in. A couple of minutes later he located the email he had sent, and confirmed he had called in, but it had been stressful. "My heart starts pounding, I start sweating, the stress that it causes, just thinking I might have to go back to jail for not calling is something I most certainly will *not* miss."

Day 454 – 11/10/2010

Color: Orange and Blue

Dave called Sherrie and let her know he was starting a new job installing insulation. Instead of being pleased, she seemed quite put out. "How in the world are you going to manage this in addition to going to school full-time?" she asked him.

"I have all of my classes at night," he told her, not bothering to point out that he had been working for me doing cleanings since February.

"Well, it still needs to be approved," she warned him. "I'll need to know the company name and address, your supervisor, your wage, how often you are paid, and I'll have to bring it up for approval with the drug court team."

All this for a few hours of work per week. Worse, Dave had hoped to avoid explaining his legal situation to his new employer. Thankfully, the man was open-minded. He asked Dave a few questions about drug court, asked him if he was currently using, and then told him he would be happy to speak with Sherrie if she called.

Day 471 – 11/27/2010
Color: Free Day

The phone system was down, so no color for anyone today. After trying a half-dozen times, Dave called Sherrie who answered, "Hi Dave, the phone system is down; don't worry about it."

Day 474 – 11/30/2010
Color: Orange

Sherrie called, apparently incapable of simple addition. "You aren't eligible for graduation; you've only been in the program since last August," She said to Dave, "September, October, November, December, so that's only 14 months total."

Dave remained calm, "That's one year plus four months ... so, 16 months."

Sherrie's response? "Oh, right, what was I thinking? Okay well, the team will discuss it on Friday."

God save us all from public servants.

Day 478 – 12/4/2010
Color: Blue

At the NA meeting tonight there were two new attendees. A couple engaged to be married, ages 25 and 26, with three children between them, busted for 26 marijuana plants. The children are all in state custody, and include a seven-year-old with severe Asperger's and a two-year old.

According to the couple, they have no criminal record and are both being charged with Class A felonies. The prosecutor has already informed their lawyer that they intend to press for incarceration instead of the option for drug court.

The children, now in state custody, can be put up for adoption at any time. The authorities are keeping them in a children's shelter and the seven-year-old with Asperger's is being left untreated. The woman claimed that she knew nothing about the plants – that her boyfriend had his 'man cave' down in the basement and that he kept it padlocked.

Day 481 – 12/7/2010
Color: Blue

Dave called Sherrie and asked her if the team had decided on a graduation date yet. She told him that the team had "been too busy" with other things and didn't get around to it. "You'll probably graduate sometime in January," she said, "but we haven't discussed a date yet." In other words, a big FUCK YOU from the drug court team.

Day 483 – 12/9/2010
Color: Yellow and Blue

Wednesday night was group therapy in Harrisonville with a new psychologist on the team. She said she was not part of the drug court team and therefore anything they said in group, as long as the individual did not appear to be at risk for relapsing, was completely confidential and would go no further than that room.

What followed was a two-hour bitch session from the group of attendees, predominantly Phase Fours, who had a lot to say about the drug court team, none of it flattering.

One of the attendees began to cry. During the time she had been in the program, both her mother and her father had passed away. Through her tears, she recalled one of the team members saying to her, "We don't care if your mother died."

Someone else brought up how the judge had ripped up Dave's business plan in court and tossed the pieces in the air. There were many stories, and a great deal of anger. The new doctor listened, and commiserated, "It is regrettable that you should have to lie, just to get through the program, especially when they stress honesty."

Dave came back from Treatment that night noticeably lighter; it had felt good to share with others.

Day 484 – 12/10/2010
Color: Yellow and Phase Four

Stockholm syndrome flared up at Treatment. At least three of the individuals in the Wednesday night class called and told a drug court team member every detail of what was discussed in the Wednesday night treatment. It caused a loud debacle and Dave was told that his application has been rejected and that he needed to re-write and re-submit it.

One of the counselors, Sonia, gave him some good advice. She said, "Tell the truth, even if it isn't what we want to hear. If you haven't gotten anything out of drug court, then say that."

Dave came home late that night from class and began to draft a new paper. "I need your help with this," he said.

"I'll be happy to help, but I am not at the top of my game right now." I responded. "It's nearly 11 p.m. Let me get some sleep. You write what you can, then email it to my computer. I'll get up at 5 a.m. and review it and make edits." It wasn't the answer he had hoped to hear, but he agreed.

Day 485 – 12/11/2010
Color: No Action

As promised, I was up by 5 a.m. with a clear head. I'm definitely a morning person. I read over what he had written and quickly realized what I needed to do. I shifted a great deal of the added verbiage to a new section and then clarified some of his writing. I knew what he wanted to say.

When I had most of it finished, I woke him up and we read over it. He hugged me, "Thank you hon; that was just what I needed!"

Here is what he submitted to the drug court time, just in time for the weekly meeting ...

How long have you been in Drug Court?

I have been in Drug Court for 16 months in December. I started on August 13th, 2009.

How long have you been clean and sober?

I stopped smoking marijuana in November 2008 and have not had a drink since July 2009. At the writing of this paper, I have 484 days clean.

Name of Employer:

I teach Tai Chi classes in North Kansas City through my company Kansas City Chi Gung. I am considering starting another company that builds and installs insulated boxes around attic fans. That company is called Attic Boxes.

I am working for a home insulation company called Millennium Insulation. We insulate homes and businesses in the Kansas City area with blow-in cellulose and expanding foam insulation. We were given an award in 2009 for a building that we insulated. It had the greatest increase in energy efficiency of any building done that year.

When I am not working for Millennium, I help out my wife, cleaning houses. Her company is called C's Cleaning Services.

Do you have a GED or High school diploma?

Yes, I graduated from high school in 1987 from the Independent Learning School in San Francisco, California.

How long have you been at this job?

I have been teaching Tai Chi for 10 years. I have worked for my wife for 4 years. Attic Boxes is brand new, as is my employment at Millennium Insulation.

Who do you live with?

I live with my wife and our daughter. Our older daughter lives in San Jose, California.

Is this a sober living environment?

Yes. My wife does not drink or use drugs.

What have you learned while you have been in drug court?

Addiction is a disease, not in the exact way that Diabetes is a disease, but for this example, the analogy will work. If someone is diabetic and either does not know they are or refuses to admit that they are, they are powerless over the disease. If they admit that they have this condition, they must re-educate themselves, changing what and when they eat, how much exercise they get, etc. Addicts must be similarly re-educated in how they deal with stress, impulse control, associations, etc.

The First Step says that we must admit that we were powerless over our addiction and that our lives had become unmanageable. In the second step, we find that there is a program that can teach us how to act on our impulses and in the third step we pledge to dedicate ourselves to that program. From that point, from the moment of commitment in step 3, we are on a road which can remove the powerlessness of the addiction, and put us back in the driver's seat of our lives again. In that way, I believe that I am not powerless over my addiction. I have found that power and I have the character tools to choose to stay sober and in recovery. I did not get this from Drug Court but from NA.

How has Drug Court helped you?

If it had not been for Cass County Drug Court, I would be in prison. Instead, I get to watch my daughter grow up and be present in her life first hand rather than just in pictures and occasional visits. The thought of having to experience prison and then living the rest of my life with a felony hanging over my head was a grim prospect indeed. I understand that my selfish actions put me in this position, and I am truly grateful for the opportunity for rehabilitation.

I was obligated to go to NA, something that I would not have done on my own. There, I saw that I could live a sober life. I saw people like myself who had made the choice to live without drugs.

In a very serious way, Drug Court was the stick and NA was the carrot. At first, I was only going to NA because of the sanctions that would be imposed if I disobeyed. NA showed me a new way to live. Sort of like the old saying, "You can lead a horse to water, but you can't make him drink," I was forced to *go to NA, but I embraced sobriety myself with the help of my NA family. It is easy to make people abstain from using, but embracing sobriety is a personal choice.*

When I was advanced to Phase Four, Judge Baker gave me a magnet with the message, "Be the change you want to see in the world". I have reflected on this quote and see that it connects to several aspects of my life. It is the same idea as the middle part of the Serenity Prayer, "Grant me the courage to change the things I can." We are only as good as our actions, not our intentions.

We need to ask ourselves how our actions fit into the Golden Rule. Would we be satisfied with someone else if they treated us the way we are treating them? How can we live our lives with less lies? What can we do today to be better people? How can we stop judging others for what we perceive as their shortcomings? How can we all be the change we want to see in the world?

What are your plans for the future?

Recovery: I will continue to work with my sponsor on a weekly basis, discussing our weeks, family, work, etc. I plan on continuing to attend NA meetings as often as possible and offer guidance to new members, giving support where I can and referring them to more experienced members when needed.

Family: I will continue to work on my relationship with my wife and daughters. We read to each other several nights a week and are heavily involved in our homeschool group. Christine is more involved than I am until I am out of the program and can attend events with P.E. Christine and I are researching permaculture and planning ways to make our home more ecologically stable, reduce our carbon footprint, and become more self-sufficient.

Education and Career: I am in school at the Metropolitan Community College and am on my way to getting my Associates of Science degree with a certificate in Photovoltaic Systems Design and Installation.

After that I plan to go to a 4-year college and get my Bachelors of Applied Science. I have been talking to several of the local solar companies in the Greater Kansas City area and hope to build a career with one of them.

Teaching/Spirituality: I have a few dedicated students who have asked me to teach traditional Taoist meditation. My teacher in California has just offered a comprehensive "distance learning course" including numerous CDs, DVDs, on-line discussions, and live seminars. It is something that I have been working on for 20 years. I can now delve deeper into the depth and meaning of my life.

Social life: I don't associate with old friends who use. I have a small group of friends who are supportive and whose children are a positive influence on P.E.

In general, I am a homebody. I don't go out at night. Most of my activities are based from my home.

What plans have you made for after-care once you leave Drug Court?

Please see my proposed After Care Plan.

In Addition

On Thursday morning, I was allowed to spend a few hours talking first with Labels and then with Sonia about my graduation application. They gave me some great feedback and suggestions. Sonia had a piece of advice that I am going to run with: write the unfiltered truth. It might not be what you expect in a drug court graduation application, but here we go.

My stress levels are through the roof. I am chomping at the bit to be out of the program. I described it to Sonia as similar to a long plane flight. While the flight is in the air, there is nothing to do but wait. You go through the motions, think about you what you will do after you are off the plane and can get back to your activities. There is nowhere to go and nothing to do. After the plane is on the ground, but before the "fasten your seatbelt" light goes off, everyone gets antsy. They cannot wait to be off the plane and on their way. Then, when the doors open up, everyone is jockeying to get their bags from the overhead compartment, stress levels on high. I am at the end of Phase Four, waiting for the doors to open.

    I want to be able to go to a movie in Power and Light without having to call someone for permission. I want to be able to see my parents in California without a team voting on whether or not they think it is a good idea. I do not want to have to worry about sleeping too soundly and missing a tracker visit. I am sick and tired of peeing in a cup. **I want to graduate.**

    During group on Wednesday night I described being in drug court like living with an abusive parent. I said abusive, but unstable is far more accurate. We come into court and try to judge the mood of the team. Will we be yelled at or singled out? There is no way of telling. Are they in a good mood, ready to tell jokes, or are they in a mood where the wrong word will get you reprimanded? Will they be glad that you are doing well and building a new life for yourself or will they rip up your business plans in front of your face 'just to make a point?' Will they hold you back from up phasing just to 'see how you react?'

Item #3 of the Program Goals in the Drug Court Manual (page 2) states that it should "Provide a treatment Program that is beneficial to participants, not just punishment." That sounds like rehabilitation to me, but instead, what we get is a strange hybrid. From the Treatment center, there is some level of rehabilitation, but from the drug court team there remains a firmly embedded model of incarceration, retaliation, and retribution. Always the threat of what will happen if we step out of line looms over us.

I do not feel that I have gotten any benefit from this program since I became Phase Four in July. Quite honestly, it feels like the last 5 months have been a waste of time. I also do not feel that I have benefited from either my one-on-one or Family counseling sessions. If I have issues, I go to my sponsor or to my Dad, not Labels. I am not saying that no one gets any value from Phase Four, just that I did not. In a great sense, this is also very good news. I have a wonderful support system in place and it will serve me well, long after I have left the program.

I feel that I have, in good faith, done all that has been asked of me. I have abided by the terms and conditions imposed by drug court; I have learned from the experience and I have stayed clean and sober.

The purpose of drug court is to rehabilitate. Per Merriam-Webster, the definition of rehabilitate is "to restore or bring to a condition of health or useful and constructive activity." Before I began drug court, I was only employed part-time, working for my wife and her cleaning business. I had stopped smoking marijuana, but was still drinking. Now, over sixteen months later, I am working full-time. I am involved in NA, and maintain a social life with friends who do not use drugs or alcohol. I am heavily involved in our youngest child's homeschool group. I am in school full-time and I have a specific degree goal.

In other words, my days are filled with useful and constructive activities. I have no interest in returning to the place I was in before. Instead, I look forward to leaving the program, moving on with my life, and dedicating more of my time to my family, school, and work. In this way, drug court has been an unmitigated success. I hope that the drug court team will agree and allow my graduation to go forward.

Later that day as I drove away from my second cleaning, I saw that I had a message on my cell phone. Dave's voice had a joyful note to it, "Hey babe, I heard back from the team. I had been on pins and needles and figured they would either throw me in jail or give me a graduation date." He paused for a moment, "Well ... it looks like I will graduate on January 5th!"

It's nice to know that sometimes the truth actually *does* work.

Day 503 – 12/29/2010
Color: Green and Phase Four

Dave went by the Probation and Parole department in Belton to drop a UA. While there he spoke with Sherrie, who asked him if he was excited to be graduating. "I'm looking forward to spending more time with work, school and family," he replied. "Why, are you looking forward to getting rid of me?"

Sherrie smiled and said, "Actually, except for a few hiccups, you are one of the most honest individuals I have ever seen in the program. I haven't had to worry about what you might be up to, or how you might be being sneaky."

This, despite all of the accusations from her over the past year and a half – direct or inferred. I know that as a law enforcement officer, Sherrie must be disappointed again and again by people who she hopes have changed their ways. But still, she is like so many of the officials I have encountered over the years. They are all sure you are guilty and quite unapologetic when your innocence is proven. It is as if they simply chalk it up to, "Well, I didn't get you on *this* crime, but I'm sure you are guilty of *something*." That kind of judgmental behavior still disgusts me.

Day 509 – 1/4/2011
Color: Green and Blue

The Lead Prosecutor called the house today and informed Dave that he needed to meet with him on Wednesday, prior to court. Apparently, this is to go over and sign the necessary paperwork that will finalize Dave's case and dismiss all charges. The meeting in court with the judge is the final act and she will formally announce that all charges have been dropped.

Dave was a little nervous when he got the call and asked the prosecutor if he was in trouble for having told the truth in his drug court application. The prosecutor told him that no, he didn't have any problem with what Dave had written, although he knew some members had been offended and suggested some form of retribution.

Day 510 – 1/5/2011
Color: No Action

Drug Court called today and informed Dave he had a balance of $72.50 owed that he would need to pay today. In the past, attendees have owed balance or been unable to pay their balances on graduation day, and then the court has never received the money.

I had a good laugh at the total amount, just $72.50 owed. Early on, due to frustration over the clerk not doing her job and neglecting to update the balances for months at a time, I started an Excel spreadsheet and logged each week in each Phase. The weekly fees varied, depending on the phase Dave was currently in. And by the time he reached Phase Four they charged only $10 per week, but he had to also pay $12.50 per UA, which of course, varied. My total in Excel showed a total of $155 owed, not $72.50. But why give the court extra money if they are incapable of keeping good financial records? Thank you, Candy Joe! Her incompetence had ensured we saved $82.50 in court fees. And we were struggling ... so every penny counted.

    I had been thrilled to see that she had lost the local election in November. Before that, it appeared that she didn't bother to do her job for at least two months prior. There had been no updates to the balance since then.

Day 511 – 1/6/2011 - Graduation Day!

Color: Blue and Green (and Dave still had to drop)

    I'll admit it – I cried when they called him up there and made it official. I couldn't help it. I was so incredibly relieved. Finally, *finally*, we were free. We had survived, relatively intact, with some semblance of dignity, some level of our integrity still intact. Our ordeal was finally over.

Still Standing

> "The war on drugs has been a disaster. It was a dumb idea to begin with, much like fighting fire ants with bombs. The "cure" is worse than the disease." – Joe C.

On Wednesday, January 5th, 2011, Dave graduated from the Cass County Drug Diversion program. A week later his name was expunged from the local Case.net records and he could now rest easy during most background checks. He had avoided being sent to prison for up to 25 years, successfully completed one of the most intensive drug treatment programs in the country, and managed to do it with most of his sanity and at least a tiny portion of his self-respect intact.

All in all, he spent 511 days in the program and was required to provide a urine sample for urinalysis at least 128 times (an average of one drop every four days). He spent a total of 72 hours in the county jail after forgetting to call in for his color three separate times.

Days in Phase One: 85 days, 25 UA drops

Days in Phase Two: 118 days, 36 UA drops

Days in Phase Three: 120 days, 49 UA drops

Days in Phase Four: 188 days, 18 UA drops

A few months ago I asked Dave, "What is the message you think should come from our experiences, from this book?"

He thought about it for a moment and said, "I think that for some individuals who truly battle with addiction, then NA and AA, even counseling can really help. Given the time away from drugs, given the support of others, they can change their lives. But for a pot smoker? It simply isn't going to work. Pot smoking is a *choice*, not an *addiction*."

The Truth and the Lies

In the first few months of the program, my dad said, "I would never admit I was an addict, no matter what they did to me. They could keep me forever in the program and I would never, ever give them the satisfaction of hearing those words."

When faced with the choice of participating in a drug court program or spending the next five to 15 years of your life in prison, what would you do? Would you tell the truth? Or would you lie and say you were an addict?

As Dave and I discussed the possibility of me actually publishing this book he said, "I was forced, *forced* to lie, over and over and over. To say I was an addict when I was not. If I hadn't, I would have never been allowed to graduate from the program. I would even possibly have been incarcerated."

I believe that Dave made the right choice. He also chose to participate fully in the drug court program and to learn from it what he could. He reached out to others, volunteered at times to give rides or to simply *listen* to an individual in a time of acute need. In order to survive and progress through the different phases and eventually emerge from the program, he lied and stated hundreds, if not thousands of times, that he was an addict.

This was at odds with the expectation of honesty that the program officials continued to preach each day. To this day we both believe in our hearts that Dave is not, nor ever has been, an addict of marijuana. It was a method of survival and coping. In order to successfully complete each Phase and eventually graduate, he did have to say these things. *He had to lie.* It was one of the few moral concessions he made and certainly one that made sense. He saw it as a choice between being honest and being true to his family. P.E. and I needed him, *out* of prison, and he did what he had to do to make sure he was there for us.

After 511 days in the program, and hundreds of hours of introspection, Dave had come to a very clear definition of his use of drugs and alcohol. "I don't believe I am an addict," he said one evening, "But I do believe I engage in compulsive behavior. Yes, at times I have abused alcohol and drugs. I think that for the rest of my life, before I decide to drink a beer or even think of smoking pot, I will ask myself first, 'Why am I doing this? Is it to take my mind off a disappointing day? Is it to excess?'"

Money Struggles

Due to the stringent requirements of Phase One, the invasive demands of drug court officials, and our own bad choices, we were forced to declare full Chapter 7 bankruptcy seven months into the program. We struggled to make ends meet and keep our house. We depended upon family members, food stamps, local displaced worker programs, and federal student aid programs to survive until Dave had finished with the drug court program and regained his freedom.

We tied ourselves to state and federal programs and laid bare our bank accounts and other financial information in order to continue to receive the help we so desperately needed. The independent and private part of me hated every minute of it, but we did what we had to in order to get back on our feet and continue to care for our child.

At the time of this writing, nearly seven years have passed since his graduation. A week after graduating from drug court, Dave smoked marijuana for about a week. After he had run through what a friend had given him, I asked him, "So what now?"

He looked at me and said, "Now I stop." Nearly five years would go by before he returned to indulging on any kind of a regular basis.

Dave has also returned to the IT field. It might not be the career he is hoping for, but it pays the bills.

In December 2012, Dave saw a baggie lying on the ground near a gas pump. It was filled with a half-smoked joint and what appeared to be weed. He picked it up and tossed it into the trash. Could an addict have done that?

I still run my cleaning business part-time, I teach community education classes and I am working on getting my writing career off of the ground. Except for one year in public school I have continued to homeschool my daughter and we have become foster parents for the first time to a beautiful little preschool age girl.

Our marriage and commitment to each other is stronger than ever, despite the adversity we encountered. We have continued to expand our organic gardening practices in our new home in historic Kansas City. Soon that yard will also be filled with perennials, wild edibles, fruit trees, and more.

I write in four blogs – *The Deadly Nightshade*, a blog that covers organic gardening and self-sufficiency topics, *The Learning Advocate*, a blog that discusses parenting and education issues, *ChristineShuck.com* – my author website/blog, and *The CottageBB* – a blog detailing our experiences renovating two homes and an RV to turn into Airbnb destinations.

My readership on both blogs grows each day. I have written a total of six books (as of late 2017) with more on the way.

In early May 2012 we heard from one of the counselors at drug court, Sonia. She told us that they had received funding to start a community garden in Belton, and was asking for some advice/help on getting started. Dave met with her and a local Master Gardener, and Sonia later came by our house, where we gave her a smorgasbord of fresh organic produce to try, along with some freshly harvested honey. We shared freely of our knowledge of composting and companion planting techniques and remain committed to supporting the group in their gardening endeavors as our busy schedules allow.

We remain committed to the belief that marijuana use:
- Is *not* immoral
- Should *not* be illegal
- Is *not* addictive.

We welcome the day when the laws of this land reflect the will of the people instead of bowing to the financial and political incentives of locking thousands of non-violent drug offenders away in prisons. We live in a nation that cares more about incarcerating a non-violent drug offender than they do about removing a pedophile from doing direct harm to an innocent child. How does that make any kind of sense?

The War on Drugs has taken innocent people's lives, turned others into snitches and informants (which in turn has often cost those people their lives), and it has ripped apart countless families. It is an *immoral* war. It is about money; it is about control – clothed in the purported guise of saving people from themselves. Its proponents and officers carry with them the misguided insistence that individuals are so stupid, so helpless in their addiction that it is better to incarcerate them, demean them, and strip them of their freedom and their free will rather than let their drug use continue.

If we as a nation want to make a real change for the better, it should be to legalize marijuana, to remove the non-violent drug offenders from prison and rehabilitate them back into society, where they can return to their families and create lives with purpose. It is my sincere hope that we will see that reality come to pass in the near future. The tide is turning, our voices must be heard, and our futures radically changed.

Someday I hope I can say the following.

"In time, this war - like every other war - ended." – Red Dawn, 1984

The tide *is* turning; I hope I get to say it soon.

Eleven Years Later: The March Forward Continues

> "Sounds to me like if we legalize and tax weed, we end up with a win-win. Nobody goes to jail for it any longer (other than DUI/"high and disorderly" sort of offenses) so we save there.
> Taxes can be earmarked for schools, rehab programs for the kind of drugs that actually DO hurt people disproportionately. Works for me." - S.B.

In late 2017, I decided to revisit this book, add some more details and corrections to needed areas, and take a moment to really review how far we, as a nation, have come.

At the time, this map depicted significant progress as more and more states moved into legalizing medical marijuana and/or legalizing recreational marijuana.

Information is current as of Sept. 14, 2017.

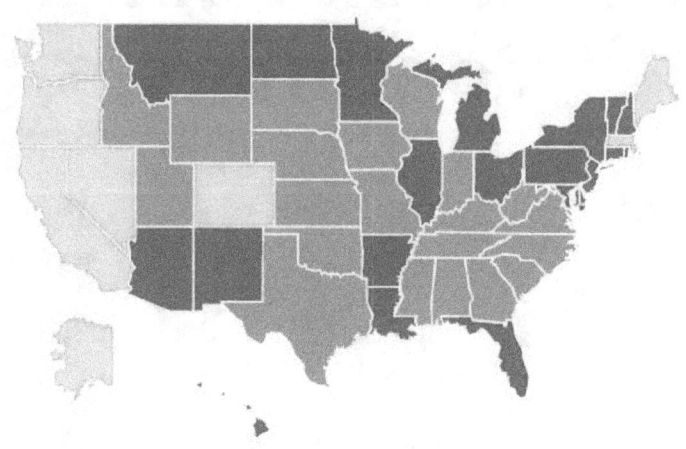

Marijuana Legalization Status
- Medical marijuana broadly legalized
- Marijuana legalized for recreational use
- No broad laws legalizing marijuana

This map is exciting and frustrating at the same time. I'm happy to see a large number of states moving into the green zones. Unfortunately for us, our home state of Missouri was not one of them.

Today's map is very different:

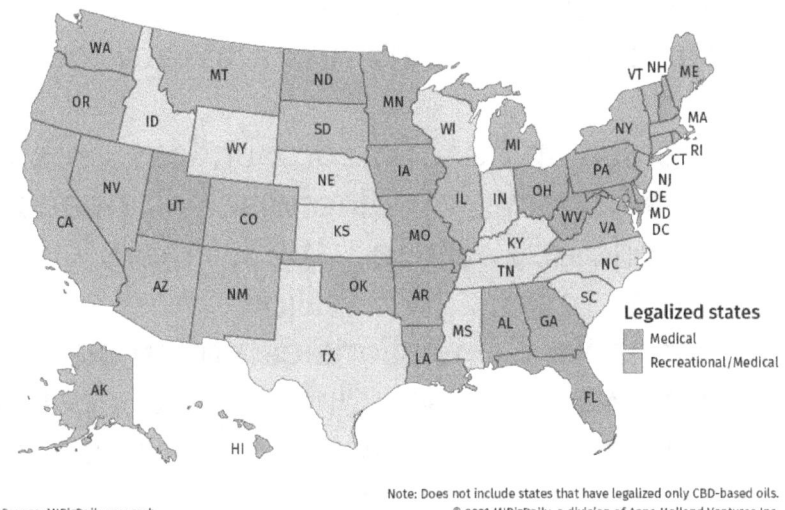

Dozens of states now allow medical marijuana and/or recreational and it is an amazing change. That said, our fight is not over. It won't be over until marijuana is legalized on a federal level. Until then, these changes, while wonderful, create a schism between federal and state governments. In early 2019, the day he introduced the Marijuana Justice Act, (S.597) Senator Cory Booker (D-NJ) tweeted, "The failed War on Drugs has really been a war on people—disproportionately criminalizing poor people, people of color & people with mental illness. I'm reintroducing the #MarijuanaJustice Act to begin reversing our failed federal drug policies."

The reasons for legalizing marijuana on a national level are many. Let's take a look at them.

- Prohibition has ruined countless lives by incarcerating otherwise peaceful Americans. Since 1995, there have been over 15 million arrests for cannabis. Convictions can often stand in the way of securing a job, getting housing, receiving professional licensure, student loans, food assistance, or firearms permits.
- Cannabis is safer than alcohol. Research has consistently proved that it is less toxic, has less potential for addiction and is less likely to contribute to serious medical problems.
- A country that values liberty should not be punishing adults for using cannabis. We live in a nation that spouts the well-worn adage of "life, liberty, and the pursuit of happiness" and the government should not be destroying lives and families over a plant that has less deleterious affects than alcohol.
- Focusing on cannabis offenders prevents the police from focusing on real crime. Their focus should be on helping prevent rape, robberies, burglaries and other violent crimes.

- Cannabis laws are racially disproportionate. As I mentioned earlier in the book, black Americans are far more likely to be arrested for cannabis possession than white Americans are. To the tune of 3.5 times as often. This is unacceptable.
- Prohibition wastes public resources, whereas legalizing and taxing marijuana brings in revenue. We could take that revenue and dedicate it to treating true addiction and help millions of Americans who are addicted to narcotics.

And that's just a few reasons.

If the stories related in this book, and by countless others have troubled or angered you, then I urge you to get involved by voting your conscience and working toward a future free of prohibition and incarceration.

Acknowledgments

For all of those who have been victimized by the War on Drugs – some of whom have been incarcerated, and those who have shared their stories with me (many of whom did not make the pages of this book), I thank you for your time, your experiences, and your sharing.

And I simply could not have written this book without the opportunity of an up close, in-depth observation of an actual drug court (and its officers, judges, deputies, and counselors) in action. Seeing and experiencing the behaviors of all involved was an eye-opening experience. It clarified my understanding of the process and how they felt about drug court attendees as individuals, as unworthy of common courtesy or any modicum of respect. I saw first-hand how those accused of drug offenses are categorized and labeled countless times.

Thanks also to my friends who were kind enough to read this book and share their thoughts.

Finally, this book would not be possible without the love and commitment of my family, both near and far. To my children and to my husband David, whose patience and love brings out the best in me.

[1] Stanford Prison Experiment, http://www.prisonexp.org/ (1999-2012)
[2] ProCon, *Historical Timeline*, http://medicalmarijuana.procon.org/view.resource.php?resourceID=000143 (8 June 2012).
[3] 420 Magazine, *Modern Uses for the Cannabis Plant*, http://www.420magazine.com/forums/hemp-facts-information/78024-modern-uses-cannabis-plant.html (1 July 2008).
[4] Judge James P. Gray, *Why Our Drug Laws Have Failed and What We Can Do About It* (Philadelphia: Temple University Press, 2001), 168
[5] Drug War Rant, *Why Is Marijuana Illegal?*, http://www.drugwarrant.com/articles (2012)
[6] The Washington Post, *Dr. Bronner's Magic Soaps CEO arrested in hemp protest*, http://www.washingtonpost.com/local/dr-bronners-magic-soaps-ceo-arrested-in-hemp-protest/2012/06/11/gJQAhwLwUV_story.html (11 June 2012)
[7] Judge James P. Gray, *Why Our Drug Laws Have Failed and What We Can Do About It* (Philadelphia: Temple University Press, 2001), 96
[8] Freeman, Morgan. *Breaking the Taboo*, DVD. Directed by Cosmo Feilding Mellen and Fernando Grostein Andrade. Los Angeles: Sundog Pictures, 2011.
[9] World Prison Population List 8th Edition, http://www.prisonstudies.org/info/downloads/wppl-8th_41.pdf (2008)
[10] Lester Grinspoon, M.D.& James B. Bakalar, J.D. "The War on Drugs – A Peace Proposal" *New England Journal of Medicine* 330 (February 1994): 357–360.
[11] Federal Bureau of Investigation. "Crime in the United States," Washington, D.C.: Government Printing Office, 1991.
[12] Freeman, Morgan. *Breaking the Taboo*, DVD. Directed by Cosmo Feilding Mellen and Fernando Grostein Andrade. Los Angeles: Sundog Pictures, 2011.
[13] Color Lines, *Masked Racism: Reflections on the Prison Industrial Complex*, http://colorlines.com/archives/1998/09/masked_racism_reflections_on_the_prison_industrial_complex.html (10 September 1998)
[14] Rania Khalek, *21st Century Slaves: How Corporations Exploit Prison Labor*, http://www.alternet.org/world/151732/21st-century_slaves%3A_how_corporations_exploit_prison_labor/?page=entire (21 July 2011)
[15] Judge James P. Gray, *Why Our Drug Laws Have Failed and What We Can Do About It* (Philadelphia: Temple University Press, 2001), 125
[16] National Institute of Justice, *Drug Courts: The Second Decade*, http://www.nij.gov/pubs-sum/211081.htm (June 2006)
[17] The National Association of Drug Court Professionals Drug Court Standards Committee, *Defining Drug Courts: Ten Key Components*, (1997, January). U.S. Department of Justice Office of Justice Programs.
[18] Democrat Missourian, *For Some This Is What Justice Should Look Like*, http://www.demo-mo.com/2011/12/30/16588/prosecutor-for-some-this-is-what.html (30 December 2011)
[19] Democrat Missourian, *People Can Change and It Is Happening Every Day*, http://www.demo-mo.com/2011/11/19/16227/people-can-change-and-its-

happening.html (19 November 2011)

[20] Psychology Today, *Is Marijuana Addictive?*, http://www.psychologytoday.com/blog/the-teenage-mind/201012/is-marijuana-addictive (5 December 2010)

[21] Freeman, Morgan. *Breaking the Taboo*, DVD. Directed by Cosmo Feilding Mellen and Fernando Grostein Andrade. Los Angeles: Sundog Pictures, 2011.

[23] Drug Policy Alliance. *Drug Courts Are Not the Answer: Toward a Health-Centered Approach to Drug Use.* http://www.drugpolicy.org/sites/default /files/Drug%20Courts%20Are%20Not%20the%20Answer_Final2.pdf (March 2011)

www.ingramcontent.com/pod-product-compliance
Lightning Source LLC
Chambersburg PA
CBHW070722240426
43673CB00003B/105